MOTHERWELL FC
On This Day

MOTHERWELL FC
On This Day

*History, Facts & Figures
from Every Day of the Year*

DEREK WILSON

MOTHERWELL FC
On This Day

History, Facts & Figures from Every Day of the Year

All statistics, facts and figures are correct as of 1st September 2008

© Derek Wilson

Derek Wilson has asserted his rights in accordance with the Copyright, Designs and Patents Act 1988 to be identified as the author of this work.

Published By:
Pitch Publishing (Brighton) Ltd
A2 Yeoman Gate
Yeoman Way
Durrington
BN13 3QZ

Email: info@pitchpublishing.co.uk
Web: www.pitchpublishing.co.uk

First published 2008

10-digit ISBN: 1-9054113-7-5
13-digit ISBN: 978-1-9054113-7-5

Printed and bound in Great Britain by Cromwell Press

ACKNOWLEDGEMENTS

It would have been impossible to take on this project without reference to a number of excellent books on Motherwell which have already been published. *A History of the Steelmen* by John Swinburne, *The Men Who Made Motherwell* by Jim Jeffrey and Genge Fry, *'Well Again* by Graham Barnstaple and Keith Brown and *Motherwell Champions of Scotland* by Alex Smith were all valuable sources of information. James Reid's website motherwellfc.org provided a wonderful news archive of more recent events while the Motherwell Heritage Centre's collection of local newspapers dating back to the 19th century proved crucial.

My father, John, was an able and willing research assistant and both my parents contributed hours of proofreading. Any mistakes which slipped through the net are entirely my responsibility and but for their help there would have been many more. Keith Brown was a great help in checking facts about older players while John Swinburne provided access to his huge archive of pictures, currently held at the Scottish Football Museum, who could not have been more helpful in providing access. I would also like to thank Alan Burrows of Motherwell Football Club for his assistance and Dan Tester at Pitch Publishing for the opportunity to write this book. Finally Anne Muras, my long suffering girlfriend, who put up with weeks of neglect and bad temper with more understanding than I deserved.

Derek Wilson – September 2008

FOREWORD BY JOHN GOLDTHORP

Motherwell is a special club and will always have a unique place in my heart. My career took me to various teams, but for a Lanarkshire lad playing at Fir Park couldn't be beaten – my boyhood ambition had been to play for my local team. Fortunately, for the majority of my time at the club the side was successful and we enjoyed both good finishes in the league and some impressive cup runs. I watched Gordon Banks make his world-class save from Pele in 1970. Then, two months later, I scored the winning goal past him in the Texaco Cup. Despite moving on, the Motherwell score was always the first I looked for on a Saturday evening. As you will see throughout the book, the club has had some glorious highs as well as devastating lows both recently and throughout its glorious history. However, the one constant is the wonderful fans who give their time and money to follow the side around the country and even into Europe on occasion. I am proud to have worn the famous claret and amber jersey for so long but just as proud to be one of the supporters to this day.

John Goldthorp, Motherwell 1967-1976

INTRODUCTION

Motherwell On This Day follows the ups and downs of the club in the form of facts, figures and trivia for each date of the year since the club was founded in 1886.

It has been a dramatic journey throughout the 122-year history of Motherwell, the team initially formed by the merger of Alpha and Glencairn. The book begins on January 1st and winds its way out of winter, through the spring and summer months and back into the gloom of December. There are derby highs and lows at the start of the year and plenty of cup upsets – which will bring back both happy and sad memories. In April and May the league championship frequently comes to a dramatic conclusion, often with the side battling relegation. However, there have been positives, not least the arrival of the Scottish title in 1932, and various days guaranteeing European qualification. Summer is quieter but hopes and disappointments still arrive just as frequently as players and managers come and go. August brings a fresh start before the gritty winter months return and, of course, there are tales of heroism on the park and near disaster off it sprinkled throughout.

The phrase 'labour of love' is the perfect summation for the book. Many educational hours were spent pawing over excellent books by Graham Barnstaple and Keith Brown, John Swinburne and Alex Smith while ancient programmes were searched out from all manner of dusty locations to provide crucial details. The Heritage Centre in Motherwell also proved to hold a mine of information. The book was a huge challenge but thoroughly enjoyable and I can only wish you the same pleasure in reading as I had in writing it.

Derek Wilson – September 2008

MOTHERWELL FC
On This Day

JANUARY

TUESDAY 1st JANUARY 1935

'Well kicked off with a traditional Ne'erday derby but were not made welcome first-footers at Hamilton. The Accies dished out a 6-1 hammering as Motherwell twice went down to nine men. Injuries to Thomson and Stevenson saw them spend time off the park and though able to return, there was no second chance for Ellis or Wales who were sent off.

THURSDAY 1st JANUARY 1948

Motherwell defeated Airdrie 2-0 but the derby was notable for a 'one game, one goal' appearance by William Sneddon. It was his only league match in two seasons spent at Fir Park.

SATURDAY 1st JANUARY 1949

A 3-1 win at Albion Rovers marked Johnny Aitkenhead's debut for the club. He grabbed two goals and went on to become the regular outside-left in the side which would soon claim cup glory. He was a remarkable penalty taker, at one point netting 40 in succession.

THURSDAY 1st JANUARY 1987

Every dog has its day and Hamilton proved this by giving Motherwell a derby thrashing in 1987. Despite goals from Steve Kirk and Paul Smith, Hamilton triumphed 4-2 in a famous victory at Douglas Park.

MONDAY 2nd JANUARY 1928

A third consecutive five-goal haul earned a 5-1 victory over Hamilton which sent the side to the top of the Scottish league. The run ended with a loss at Falkirk next day which allowed Rangers to return to pole position, the spot they would occupy at the end of the season.

THURSDAY 2nd JANUARY 1958

John Martis and Andy Weir made their debuts in a 3-1 win over Hibernian. Martis had the unenviable task of replacing the legendary Andy Paton in defence but did so with great success, making over 300 appearances for Motherwell and being capped by Scotland. He eventually left in 1969 and would later go into management with East Fife when his playing days were over.

THURSDAY 3RD JANUARY 1963

Steve Kirk was born in Kirkcaldy. The Fifer made his Motherwell debut in 1986 and would go on to become a cult hero, enthralling and infuriating in equal measure throughout his nine years at Fir Park. He scored in every round of the successful 1991 cup run and remains the club's top scorer in European competition with five goals.

MONDAY 3RD JANUARY 1983

Two unlikely points in the battle against relegation arrived when Rangers were destroyed 3-0 at Fir Park. Young striker Brian McClair put himself firmly in the shop window with his hat-trick and soon moved to Celtic, then Manchester United, where he picked up several honours and international caps.

TUESDAY 3RD JANUARY 1989

Motherwell bade farewell to one of the grand old grounds of Scottish football with a defeat. Hamilton Academical triumphed 2-0 in the last derby at Douglas Park but it wasn't enough to keep them in the Premier League. The stadium site is now a supermarket with Accies' new home being built just a few hundred yards from the original location.

SATURDAY 3RD JANUARY 2004

Phil O'Donnell donned the claret and amber once more, nearly ten years after his record £1.75m transfer to Celtic. He came off the bench in this 3-1 win over Dundee United but it was his nephew, David Clarkson, who stole the headlines. Clarkson scored a perfect hat-trick – goals with left, right and head – in the second half to secure the victory.

FRIDAY 4TH JANUARY 2008

More than 500 mourners attended Phil O'Donnell's funeral at St Mary's church in Hamilton. Several famous faces from football north and south of the border were present to pay their respects, as were hundreds of fans who gathered outside to hear the service through loudspeakers. O'Donnell had died of heart failure just six days earlier after collapsing on the pitch in a match against Dundee United.

SATURDAY 5TH JANUARY 2002

The Scottish Cup campaign lasted only one game as the side surrendered meekly in a 3-1 defeat at Dunfermline Athletic. Motherwell were never in the contest and scored only a late consolation through Stuart Elliot when the tie was already beyond them. The popular Northern Irish winger had been left on the bench, a decision which drew a barrage of criticism from the Motherwell support. It emerged that after the game a confrontation had taken place between striker David Kelly and the management team of Eric Black and Terry Butcher. Kelly left the club shortly after the incident.

SATURDAY 6TH JANUARY 1990

Happier times at East End Park as a sensational performance resulted in a 5-0 away win. Inspired by Davie Cooper, doubles from Nick Cusack and Johnny Gahagan, along with a strike from Steve Kirk produced the first five-goal haul in the top flight since September 1977.

SATURDAY 7TH JANUARY 1956

A legend said farewell to Fir Park when Wilson Humphries played his last game for the club in a win over Stirling. Humphries remained involved with the game as a coach after his playing days ended and also taught many Motherwell stars of the future at Dalziel High School.

SATURDAY 7TH JANUARY 1989

A hilarious own goal by Richard Gough was enough to give Motherwell a 2-1 win over Rangers. Wishart had equalised early in the second half and the margin of victory could have been greater had Dave McCabe's goal not been ruled out for offside.

TUESDAY 7TH JANUARY 1997

With the side struggling at the wrong end of the Premier League, manager Alex McLeish swooped for striker Owen Coyle. Jamie Dolan, who came through the youth system in the 1980s, moved to Tannadice in exchange while Motherwell also pocketed £75,000 in the deal. Coyle would score a number of vital goals in the nerve-racking battle against the drop.

MONDAY 8TH JANUARY 1951

Months after winning the League Cup, a civic reception was organised by the town council in recognition of the achievement. The dinner was hosted by the Provost in the Town Hall and he paid tribute to players past and present. A telegram from Hibs, the defeated opposition in the final, was read, congratulating Motherwell on the 3-0 Hampden Park victory.

WEDNESDAY 8TH JANUARY 1992

One of Tommy McLean's most astute purchases arrived at Fir Park. Rob McKinnon continued the long line of excellent Motherwell left-backs after his £150,000 transfer from Hartlepool United. McKinnon was reliable in defence and strong going forward, notching a number of important goals. His fine form was recognised by Scotland and he earned three international caps. He became one of the first Motherwell players to use the Bosman ruling, leaving on a free transfer to Twente Enschede in 1996 after making over 150 appearances in claret and amber. After two years in Holland, he returned to the UK, playing briefly for Carlisle United in between spells at Hearts and Clydebank.

SUNDAY 8TH JANUARY 1995

The chase for the league title suffered a severe blow when Hearts managed to steal an undeserved victory from Fir Park. Chris McCart was prone on the ground when attempting a clearance which drifted back to 'keeper Woods in the wind but referee Louis Thow gave a pass back foul. Hearts scrambled home the free-kick for the winning goal, meaning Motherwell dropped to third on goal difference behind Hibs and 12 points behind league leaders Rangers.

SATURDAY 9TH JANUARY 1993

The remodelling of Fir Park continued after the Taylor Report as the huge South Stand opened behind the goal to accommodate away supporters. On its first day in use it was filled by 4,800 Rangers fans who saw their side ease through to the fourth round of the Scottish Cup with a simple 2-0 win.

FRIDAY 10th JANUARY 1958

Lanarkshire was devastated by bad storms and Fir Park did not escape unscathed. The high winds blew off several parts of the enclosure roof, and with it much of the floodlighting system. The weekend game against Falkirk was postponed due to debris being scattered over the playing surface.

TUESDAY 10th JANUARY 1961

The board received a quote of £32,738 from Tubewrights Ltd to build a new Main Stand at Fir Park. The existing structure was deemed too small and in need of improvement. The new construction should have been able to house 5,000 spectators but was never built the full length of the pitch due to objections from local residents. When the stand was eventually opened, some Motherwell fans boycotted the seats as they believed it had been paid for with the transfers of Ian St John and Pat Quinn to England.

SATURDAY 10th JANUARY 2004

Young Australian Scott McDonald made a scoring debut for the club in the 3-0 cup win against St Johnstone. McDonald would become a prolific scorer, netting 44 goals before making a £700,000 move to Celtic. He polarised the support with his attitude on the pitch and a string of media comments expressing his desperation for a transfer to a bigger club.

SATURDAY 11th JANUARY 1936

The BBC made the first live radio broadcast from Fir Park when *Scottish Daily Express* journalist Alan Breck provided commentary of the 1-1 draw with Clyde. John McMenemy got the goal which maintained a three-month unbeaten run but the side were always below the main title challengers and eventually finished fourth.

TUESDAY 11th JANUARY 1994

Motherwell took on Celtic in the first instalment of a January league and cup double header. The points were won with two goals from Phil O'Donnell. The second was a stunning volley and kept the side well placed in the hunt for European football.

THE MAIN STAND – NOW NAMED AFTER PHIL O'DONNELL – GETS A FACELIFT IN THE 1960s

WEDNESDAY 12TH JANUARY 1966

Motherwell legend John 'Sailor' Hunter died aged 86. Hunter had a long association with Fir Park between 1911 and 1959 and was the all-powerful manager responsible for making the club a force in the late 1920s and 1930s. A historic championship was secured in 1932 as the club spent an astonishing eight consecutive seasons in the top three. After the war, he gave up his managerial position to concentrate on secretarial duties.

SATURDAY 12TH JANUARY 2008

Charlie Aitken died aged 75. Aitken spent his whole career at Fir Park from 1949 to 1966 before being awarded a testimonial game a year later. He played in the Ancell Babes side but missed out on the 1952 Cup win due to national service. Despite representing Scotland B, and the Scottish League, he was never capped by the full national side. The immensely competitive wing-half was only ever booked once – but even then claimed the referee had got the decision wrong.

TUESDAY 13TH JANUARY 1970

The club decided to reward James Adams, the former PA announcer, with a complimentary stand ticket for life. Adams had held his position for over thirty years.

SUNDAY 13TH JANUARY 1985

Joe Wark became the first Motherwell player to be awarded a second testimonial for his service to the club. This time an Old Firm Select arrived at Fir Park to beat Motherwell 3-1, despite some guest players acting as reinforcements. The 'Well goal came from none other than Joe Jordan!

FRIDAY 13TH JANUARY 1995

A 'Friday night football' experiment took place at Fir Park when Motherwell faced Hibernian. However, both club and television viewers were disappointed with the outcome; no one will watch, regardless of when games are played, if the entertainment is as dire as this 0-0 draw! Motherwell were in the middle of a five-match run without a win which killed off the title challenge.

TUESDAY 14TH JANUARY 1992

Motherwell were held to a 3-3 draw at home to Aberdeen when Andy Roddie scored a last minute equaliser. Steve Kirk, Luc Nijholt and Phil O'Donnell were on target for the hosts. Roddie would become one of Alex McLeish's first signings in 1994 but despite possessing incredible pace and having reasonable crossing ability, the winger failed to make an impression. This strike would be the only goal he ever managed at Fir Park and, largely due to his £150,000 price tag, Roddie was widely considered one of the poorest players ever purchased by a 'Well manager.

SATURDAY 15TH JANUARY 1927

Hopes of a first championship were dashed when Rangers won 4-1 at Fir Park. The Ibrox side would eventually win the title by five points, with Motherwell coming second – the highest position achieved to date and the start of eight consecutive seasons spent in the top three.

SATURDAY 15TH JANUARY 1983

Just a couple of weeks after beating Rangers, the Old Firm 'double' was completed with victory against Celtic. Brian McClair was the goal hero once more, netting the last minute winner after Pat Bonner dropped a cross at his feet.

TUESDAY 16TH JANUARY 1996

Alex McLeish turned to Willie Falconer to end the team's goal scoring crisis and save the side from relegation. The £200,000 transfer fee seemed to be of dubious value when Falconer missed a penalty on his debut against Kilmarnock but five crucial goals helped the club pull away from the drop zone. His tally was enough to make him top scorer for the season – the lowest ever total to lead the scoring chart at Fir Park. Goals were harder to come by in the years to follow and he eventually moved on a free transfer to Dundee where he helped keep the Dens Park club in the SPL, scoring in a winning visit to Fir Park in the process.

SATURDAY 17TH JANUARY 1931

Despite Motherwell being one of the best sides in the country, local fans were notoriously picky about what games they attended. A close contest against a stronger side was much more appealing than a perceived walkover. Only a couple of thousand watched the comfortable cup victory over Bathgate on this date which started a run all the way to the final at Hampden. Perspective is given by visits from the Old Firm which attracted 30,000!

MONDAY 17TH JANUARY 1983

Despite beating Celtic the previous Saturday, manager Jock Wallace decided drastic action was needed in the fight against the drop. In the 'January sale' Hugh Sproat, Brian McLaughlin and John Gahagan were transfer listed while Bruce Cleland, Chic McClelland and Alex Forsyth were simply freed. The side eventually stayed up with room to spare, arguably justifying the bold move.

SATURDAY 18TH JANUARY 1896

The side went down to a 3-2 defeat at Renton in the Second Division. Having been elected to the league three years earlier, Motherwell struggled badly and picked up only 13 points from 18 games this season, finishing three spots from the bottom.

SATURDAY 19TH JANUARY 1991

It is largely forgotten that before the cup run started, season 1990/91 was far from inspired. A good start of impressive home form had been wasted by the winter and when the team were hammered 3-0 by Dundee United at Tannadice there was little reason to be confident about what was to come.

WEDNESDAY 19TH JANUARY 2000

One of the more bizarre stories in the club's history broke when a national newspaper claimed chairman John Boyle wanted to buy local rivals Airdrieonians and merge the clubs, creating 'Lanarkshire United' to challenge at the top of the Scottish game. Airdrie were at the beginning of the financial problems that would eventually lead to their demise but the claims were flatly denied by everyone connected with the club.

SATURDAY 20TH JANUARY 1934

Motherwell took on Gala Fairydean for the only time and ran out 4-0 winners in the Scottish Cup. Willie McFadyen scored all four goals in front of a crowd of 3,013.

FRIDAY 20TH JANUARY 1989

Willie Redpath, a Scotland international who scored in the final of the successful 1952 cup run, died on this day in 1989. It turned out to be a sad time for the club as John Johnston, the goalkeeper who played behind him, died the next day. Johnston is one of five players to have won three national finals with Motherwell, picking up a Summer Cup winners medal in 1944 along with the more well known League Cup and Scottish Cup badges in 1950 and 1952.

SATURDAY 20TH JANUARY 1990

The third round of the Scottish Cup gave the side a tricky start when Clyde visited Fir Park. A wonderful performance by the team ensured there was no slip up as the Bully Wee were dumped out 7-0. Remarkably, the seven goals came from different scorers; Chris McCart, Davie Cooper (penalty), Dougie Arnott, Steve Bryce, Bobby Russell, Steve Kirk and Johnny Gahagan all found the net. The team seemed to be finding form at just the right time, meaning a large and expectant crowd would travel to Tynecastle for the next round...

FRIDAY 21ST JANUARY 2000

After a drawn-out transfer saga, Martyn Corrigan finally signed from Falkirk for £30,000. It took some time for him to displace Michael Doesburg as the first choice right-back but eventually his Motherwell form was good enough to be rewarded with a Scotland B cap. Appropriately for a player nicknamed 'The Kaiser' it came in a match away to Germany.

SUNDAY 22ND JANUARY 2006

In an otherwise unremarkable 3-1 defeat at home to Celtic, Jim Hamilton scored one of the best goals ever seen at Fir Park – a left foot volley from twenty yards over Artur Boruc.

SATURDAY 23RD JANUARY 1954

Motherwell were stung after their first ever relegation in 1953 and wasted no time in marching back to the top flight. Several large wins were recorded in the triumphant promotion season but none more than the 12-1 demolition of Dundee United. Wilson Humphries banged in six, the biggest goal haul scored in a game by a single Motherwell player – although this record is shared with Alex Stewart and George Watson. Jackie Hunter was somewhat overshadowed with a mere four goals and Willie Redpath had just a brace. Along with being Motherwell's record win, the result remains Dundee United's heaviest defeat.

SATURDAY 23RD JANUARY 1982

Flying high at the top of the First Division, Motherwell fancied their chances when Aberdeen came to town in the Scottish Cup. Unfortunately, some slack defending allowed John Hewitt to open the scoring after a record-shattering nine seconds. An equaliser was not forthcoming despite the players' best efforts over the next 89 minutes and 51 seconds.

SATURDAY 24TH JANUARY 1976

Trailing 2-0 to Celtic at half-time in the Scottish Cup should have indicated an early exit was on the cards but instead Motherwell produced a heroic comeback. Bobby Graham and Ian Taylor pulled the side level before Willie Pettigrew raced clear to fire home the winner. On the match highlights, legendary commentator Arthur Montford described the defining moment as "a chance of a lifetime for Pettigrew" but by then, of course, everyone knew he would take it.

SUNDAY 24TH JANUARY 1999

Like all grounds, Fir Park has a special atmosphere under floodlights. The thought of an evening cup-tie against cup holders Hearts had the old stadium rocking even before Ged Brannan slammed home the opener from a well-worked set piece. Hearts equalised in the second half but goals from Owen Coyle and Tony Thomas secured one of the most memorable victories achieved under the leadership of Billy Davies.

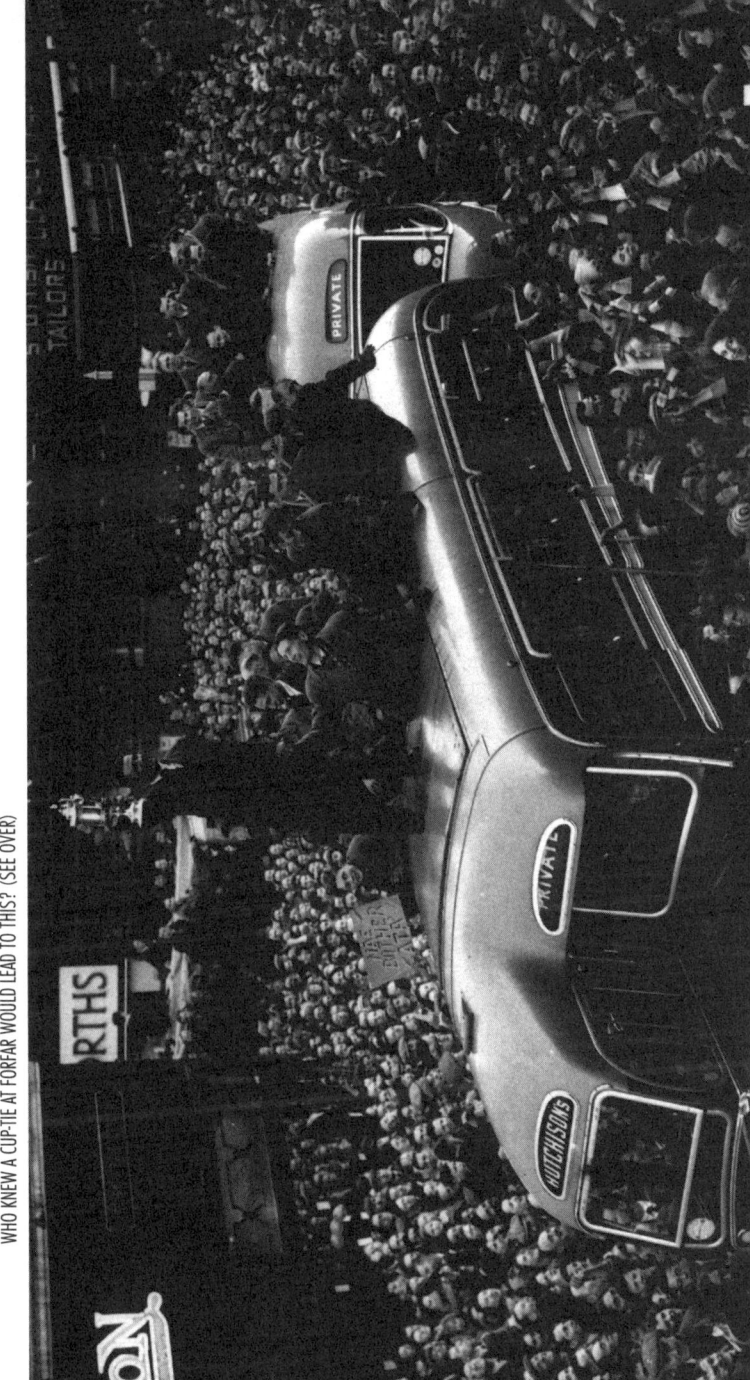

WHO KNEW A CUP-TIE AT FORFAR WOULD LEAD TO THIS? (SEE OVER)

SATURDAY 25TH JANUARY 1992

Motherwell's first defence of the Scottish Cup in 39 years started at Somerset Park. Ayr United proved stiff opposition and more than deserved the draw which earned them a replay at Fir Park. Brian Martin bundled home from close range to open the scoring but Duncan George's equaliser set up a frantic closing spell. Neither side could find a winner but it was Motherwell who strolled through the replay, winning 4-1.

SATURDAY 26TH JANUARY 1952

There would have been no reason to suspect a trip to Station Park would be the start of a glory trail but the team would finally bring the Scottish Cup back to Motherwell in 1952. Forfar were dispatched 4-2 at the start of a ten game cup run.

SATURDAY 26TH JANUARY 1991

Remarkably, the same date witnessed the beginning of the club's only other Scottish Cup triumph. Aberdeen were challenging for the league but paid the penalty for not scoring in a first half they dominated. Motherwell came back into things and, just 14 seconds after coming off the bench, Steve Kirk struck the only goal of the contest with his first touch.

TUESDAY 27TH JANUARY 1998

Having narrowly avoided a humiliating cup defeat at Dumbarton, Motherwell progressed past the Sons with a 1-0 replay win. Dumbarton missed a glorious chance to win the tie at the first attempt and turned in a second creditable performance at Fir Park, the width of a post denying them a crack at extra time.

SATURDAY 27TH JANUARY 2001

An expectant Motherwell support travelled to struggling St Mirren for a third round cup tie but things took a bad twist when Don Goodman was sent off for two dives – television evidence later showed he was tripped on both occasions. Goals from Lee McCulloch and John Spencer were enough to secure the win even though Greg Strong was also sent off with ten minutes remaining.

SATURDAY 28TH JANUARY 1967

Berwick Rangers defeated Rangers 1-0 in the most famous Scottish Cup upset of all time. Former Ancell Babe Sammy Reid scored the winner.

TUESDAY 28TH JANUARY 1969

After a draw at Fir Park, Clyde eliminated the side in a Shawfield cup replay. Motherwell were in the Second Division at the time and fought bravely before losing a last minute goal. The match was notable for the fact goalkeeper Keith McCrae played as an outfield player. He was occasionally used as a midfielder or forward in his time at the club and even notched a goal on one occasion!

THURSDAY 28TH JANUARY 1999

John Spencer became Motherwell's record signing when he arrived for £600,000 from Everton. Spenny had already completed a successful loan at the club but the transfer was a drawn-out affair. Spencer struggled to justify the fee and huge wages as a permanent signing, averaging only one goal every four games. He was allowed to join Colorado in 2001 as cost cutting started too late to prevent the club slipping into administration in 2002. Eventually, Spencer became embroiled in a legal dispute with the club over the repayment of a loan after his departure.

SATURDAY 29TH JANUARY 1972

St Johnstone were beaten 2-0 at Fir Park despite Motherwell goalkeeper Billy Ritchie going off with a broken leg. Left-back Joe Wark showed his flexibility by standing in between the posts and kept a very impressive clean sheet in more than 45 minutes of action.

SATURDAY 29TH JANUARY 2000

An epic cup battle started with Arbroath. Motherwell were leading through a Derek Townsley goal at Gayfield when referee Mike McCurry abandoned the match due to high winds whipping in from the neighbouring North Sea. After a draw in the second attempt, pitch problems at Fir Park forced the replay to be postponed on several occasions before Motherwell finally triumphed 2-0.

SATURDAY 30th JANUARY 1999

Just a week after beating Hearts in the cup, the side recorded a rare win at Tynecastle. Lee McCulloch gave the side the lead before Derek Adams completed a fine passing move with a close range finish. Spencer hit the bar on what was his debut following his permanent transfer to Lanarkshire from Everton.

WEDNESDAY 31st JANUARY 1968

Not only were Motherwell beaten in a cup replay at Airdrie, playing in a blizzard gave Jimmy Wilson flu. He missed the next game through the illness as he tried to recover.

TUESDAY 31st JANUARY 1995

Motherwell's third round cup tie at Falkirk seemed to be cursed after the second attempt at playing the game was foiled. The first date was snowed off but at least there was some action on this day before a floodlight failure caused the tie to be abandoned early in the second half. Falkirk distributed vouchers for free admittance to the rearranged game and cheeky fans promptly went to work with their photocopiers – a substantially bigger crowd finally saw Motherwell progress 2-0.

SATURDAY 31st JANUARY 1998

Alex McLeish's last game as Motherwell manager was a cracker as Hibernian were defeated 6-2. Hibs were two up inside ten minutes but trailed by half-time and were eventually on the end of a thrashing. Eric Garcin scored his only goal for the club while young Lee McCulloch finally broke his duck with a double. McLeish walked out on the side just before a cup tie with Rangers to take over at Easter Road. Despite inspiring Hibs to a win over Motherwell, McLeish couldn't save his new charges from relegation as the Steelmen survived.

THURSDAY 31st JANUARY 2008

A busy transfer deadline day saw the club swap left-backs. Jim Paterson moved to Plymouth for £250,000 while £110,000 of that was reinvested to bring Stevie Hammell back to Fir Park from Southend United.

MOTHERWELL FC
On This Day

FEBRUARY

TUESDAY 1st FEBRUARY 2005

Motherwell reached their first final in fourteen years after a sensational 3-2 League Cup semi-final victory against Hearts at Easter Road. Goals by Stephen Craigan and Richie Foran seemed to have won the tie but late strikes from Hearts with less than five minutes remaining took the game to extra time. A penalty shoot-out looked inevitable as there was little to separate the sides in the additional period... but there was drama to come. McDonald fed Fitzpatrick in the 120th minute and the young midfielder drilled his shot into the bottom corner to send the 'Well fans wild with delight.

WEDNESDAY 1st FEBRUARY 2006

Terry Butcher's side returned to Hampden to face Celtic in the semi-final of the League Cup. Richie Foran's header gave the side the lead but although Maciej Zurawski equalised, Motherwell continued to dominate. Several chances were missed before Martyn Corrigan attempted a risky back pass forcing 'keeper Graeme Smith to catch the ball. Shaun Maloney converted the 88th-minute free-kick for a 2-1 win.

SATURDAY 2nd FEBRUARY 1985

Motherwell visited Muirton Park in Perth for the last time on this day in 1985. Tommy McLean's side were battling through the First Division and a 1-0 win over St Johnstone, thanks to a goal by Ray Blair, kept them on track for promotion to the Premier League.

WEDNESDAY 2nd FEBRUARY 1994

Chris McCart was picked for a Scotland B international in Wales. The tall defender scored twice but sadly once at the wrong end as Scotland went down 2-1 to the hosts in Wrexham. McCart also represented the Scottish League but missed out on a full Scotland cap.

MONDAY 3rd FEBRUARY 1975

The travelling support at Firhill were shocked when Motherwell took the field in black and blue stripes for this cup replay. In a strip reminiscent of Inter Milan, Motherwell defeated Partick Thistle 1-0 with Willie Watson grabbing the late winner.

SATURDAY 4TH FEBRUARY 1911

Motherwell finally recorded their first competitive win over Celtic when two goals by Wattie Brand produced a 2-1 victory. A total of 9,000 fans saw the game at Fir Park as Motherwell beat the Glasgow giants at the fifteenth time of asking.

WEDNESDAY 4TH FEBRUARY 1967

The Supporters' Association annual quiz night took place on this evening. The teams had an extra incentive to do well as the winners would be entered into a further competition arranged by a local radio station.

SATURDAY 4TH FEBRUARY 1978

Entertainer Christian was introduced to the crowd before an exciting 0-0 draw with Aberdeen. The singer had been made an honorary board member and was to be responsible for adding style and glamour to the commercial department and fund raising campaigns.

SATURDAY 5TH FEBRUARY 1955

A rare visit was made to Mosset Park when the side took on Forres Mechanics in the Scottish Cup. Motherwell struggled badly against the Highland League side but eventually went through 4-3 thanks to the home side missing a last-minute penalty. The hosts also laid on a lavish civic reception at the Forres Town Hall to celebrate the visit of the top-flight side.

SATURDAY 6TH FEBRUARY 1960

BBC cameras arrived at Fir Park for the first time to film highlights of the clash with Hibernian. Despite Andy Weir scoring twice and Ian St John getting another, the visitors ran out 4-3 victors before a crowd of 12,599 in what was a superb game of football.

SATURDAY 6TH FEBRUARY 1993

Motherwell drew 0-0 at home to Airdrie in what turned out to be the last league derby between the sides at Fir Park. Airdrie held on to their point despite finishing the game with ten men. While Motherwell may have been disappointed not to win, the draw was enough to move them out of the relegation zone for the first time in months.

THURSDAY 7th FEBRUARY 1925

Former 'Well 'keeper Jock Rundell returned to Fir Park with his new side Arthurlie. However, the veteran could not prevent his old club running out 2-0 winners.

SATURDAY 7th FEBRUARY 1953

A crowd of 8,500 turned up at Recreation Park to watch Motherwell's first ever game defending the Scottish Cup. Alloa played well and the more illustrious visitors were somewhat fortunate to progress to the next round with a 2-0 win. The poor form was not surprising as Motherwell struggled badly in the league, eventually being relegated for the first time at the end of the season.

THURSDAY 8th FEBRUARY 1934

The SFA wrote to the club saying permission could not be granted for the team to take on sides selected by the national association of South Africa. Permission was given to face clubs and district sides comprising of players from the relevant jurisdiction. Motherwell frequently went on tours around this time and the money raised was vital in keeping players away from the richer teams in England.

SATURDAY 9th FEBRUARY 1952

The cup run continued at Love Street when the side travelled to face St Mirren. Things looked grim at half-time when goals from Gemmell and Wilson gave the hosts the lead against the run of play. The visitors rallied and a constant stream of pressure produced two goals for Jimmy Watson and a winner from Wilson Humphries to settle a 3-2 thriller.

SATURDAY 9th FEBRUARY 2002

David Ferrere made one of the most dramatic debuts at Fir Park when he came off the bench against Hibs. The little Frenchman had the crowd buzzing with a long-range free-kick which whizzed over the bar before he banged in three near-identical goals from the inside-right channel. Sadly Ferrere never hit the same heights and failed to score for the club again before being released a few months later.

SATURDAY 10TH FEBRUARY 1951

The attempt at the cup double continued in positive fashion when local rivals Hamilton were soundly beaten at Fir Park. A large crowd of 18,000 saw a double from Archie Kelly, along with singles from Willie Watters and Jim Forrest, see off the men from the other side of the Clyde.

SATURDAY 10TH FEBRUARY 1979

Hibs arrived at Fir Park and promptly stuffed the struggling home side 3-0. This was the start of a disastrous run of eleven games without a win which featured only three goals along the way. Relegation had been a constant threat and this kind of form did little to suggest the side deserved a top flight place.

SATURDAY 11TH FEBRUARY 1989

Motherwell recorded a famous victory at Celtic Park when Bobby Russell scored a beautiful last minute winner. John Gahagan's earlier strike had been equalised but Russell won the game with a lovely shimmy and shot into the top corner. As a former Rangers player, Russell always raised his game against the Old Firm and provided a number of useful goals from midfield. He was an important member of the 1991 cup-winning squad, scoring in the shoot-out at Morton and featuring in all but two of the seven matches; sadly for Bobby one of those games was the final. He was forced to retire due to a knee injury in 1993 while at Ayr United.

SATURDAY 12TH FEBRUARY 1994

Motherwell's European chase continued with a slightly fortuitous win at Tannadice. An inspired performance by Sieb Dykstra kept the hosts out for most of the afternoon but the Terrors proved prolific at the wrong end – Dave Bowman and Freddy van der Hoorn both headed own goals to give 'Well a 2-1 victory. It was the first win picked up at Tannadice since January 1976, ending a remarkable run of 32 games without a win on the tangerine side of Tayside.

SATURDAY 13TH FEBRUARY 1932

As Motherwell closed in on the league title, the equally elusive Scottish Cup was still being pursued. Some measure of revenge was taken against Celtic for defeat in the previous year's final when goals in either half from John Murdoch and Bobby Ferrier were enough to seal victory in front of a then-record crowd of 36,000 at Fir Park.

SATURDAY 13TH FEBRUARY 1999

Motherwell progressed to the Scottish Cup quarter-finals with an uncomfortable 2-0 win over Stirling Albion. The match provided young Bino winger Stephen Nicholas the perfect chance to showcase his skills as he gave Stephen McMillan a torrid time on the flank. Nicholas was brought to Fir Park for £100,000 but struggled to adapt to life at a bigger club and made only 14 first-team starts in over three years.

SATURDAY 14TH FEBRUARY 1903

The committee organised a fundraising smoking concert in the Lesser Town Hall. Tickets cost 6d with a number of good vocalists giving their services to contribute to a memorable night.

SATURDAY 14TH FEBRUARY 1940

Willie Hunter was born in Edinburgh. Bobby Ancell signed him from Edinburgh Norton in 1957 and he would become an integral part of the swashbuckling Motherwell side of the late 1950s and early 1960s. Hunter was a very determined player – but also exceptionally skilful – and contributed several goals, and even more assists, to the cause. Injuries hurt his career but he still collected three Scotland caps before moving on from Fir Park. He eventually played for boyhood heroes Hibs after his departure in 1967.

SATURDAY 15TH FEBRUARY 1992

The reign of the Scottish Cup holders was ended at Ibrox when Rangers defeated Motherwell 2-1. A magnificent first-half performance which saw Rangers completely outplayed produced only one long-range goal from Phil O'Donnell. The home side fought back after the break with a brace from Alexei Mikhailichenko.

SATURDAY 16TH FEBRUARY 1957

The AGM was held in the Lesser Town Hall. It was stated that unless the club took £100 income for a home game, a loss would be made.

TUESDAY 17TH FEBRUARY 1997

Motherwell were hammered 3-0 in a Scottish Cup replay at Ibrox. However, the real chance had already been missed at Fir Park when a horrific mistake by goalkeeper Stevie Woods allowed Rangers to escape with a 2-2 draw. An own goal by Richard Gough looked to have given Motherwell their first cup win over Rangers in 36 years but Stevie Woods' overly calm response to a pass back resulted in him presenting the ball to Gordon Durie for the equaliser.

THURSDAY 18TH FEBRUARY 1982

Left-back Stevie Hammell was born in Rutherglen. The defender came through the youth system at Fir Park and made over 200 appearances before joining Southend United in the summer of 2006. His welcome return in January 2008 helped Mark McGhee's team secure European football by finishing third.

SATURDAY 18TH FEBRUARY 1989

Motherwell exited the Scottish Cup after going down 2-1 to Hibs at Easter Road. The consolation goal came courtesy of Stevie Bryce, who met a clearance to send a brilliant volley flying high into the top corner. Sadly Bryce failed to fulfil his potential and was freed, joining Ayr United.

SATURDAY 19TH FEBRUARY 1994

Just a week after winning at Tannadice in the league, Motherwell returned to face Dundee United in the cup. Despite leading through Steve Kirk, a sensational double from Craig Brewster and a penalty miss from Tommy Coyne had Motherwell in trouble. John Philliben came to the rescue and lashed home an equaliser in the third minute of injury time to spark bedlam in the Motherwell enclosures. Philliben, affectionately known as Softie, was less successful in his post-match interview, famously saying he was delighted to have secured "another crack at the cherry".

SATURDAY 20TH FEBRUARY 1985

Motherwell's triumphant promotion campaign in 1985 was also matched by a good run in the Scottish Cup. A fourth round tie at Meadowbank provided few problems as a double from Andy Harrow ensured the team were in the hat for the quarter-finals. A wonderful draw presented the side with Forfar Athletic, the tie to be played at Fir Park, meaning, surely, that a first semi-final in nine years was on the cards.

SATURDAY 21ST FEBRUARY 1953

Struggling Motherwell looked to maintain their hold on the Scottish Cup in a difficult trip to Pittodrie. The side went one up but trailed Aberdeen 3-1, 4-2 and 5-3 before staging a dramatic comeback. Archie Shaw's long-range goal gave the team hope with ten minutes remaining before Charlie Cox kept the cup in Lanarkshire for a few more days by heading home a last-gasp equaliser.

TUESDAY 21ST FEBRUARY 1984

Motherwell successfully requested the game with Dundee the next day be postponed as 12 players were unavailable due to injuries and a flu bug which had swept the dressing room. The request was approved but made little difference – Dundee won the rescheduled tie 4-2 at Fir Park as the Steelmen continued their slide towards the Premier League trapdoor.

SUNDAY 21ST FEBRUARY 1999

One of the great modern-day debacles took place at Fir Park when Celtic thrashed the hosts 7-1. 'Keeper Andy Goram had been left out of the side in controversial circumstances following a newspaper exposé which showed dated pictures of him posing with flags bearing political slogans. Things took a bad turn early on when John Spencer was sent off and Stephan Mahe won a highly debatable penalty. Ged Brannan equalised but the ten men fell apart late on and Celtic ran up the score. The Motherwell fans that stayed to the end rewarded the side with a standing ovation for their efforts.

SATURDAY 22ND FEBRUARY 1930

George Stevenson became the first Motherwell player to score for Scotland when he added the clinching goal in a 3-1 win over Northern Ireland in the British International Championship. Stevenson scored three further goals for his country and remains the Motherwell player most capped for Scotland, appearing 12 times in total between 1927 and 1934. As well as being a vital part in Motherwell's glory teams in the early 1930s, Stevenson took over from John Hunter as manager in 1946 and led the team to victories in both the Scottish and League Cups.

SATURDAY 23RD FEBRUARY 1952

Motherwell fans crammed onto a football special train to Dunfermline and formed a substantial part of the 22,000-strong crowd which watched the Scottish Cup third round tie at East End Park. Willie Watson's early goal was equalised in the second half, forcing a Fir Park replay which Motherwell eventually coasted. The visitors from Fife fought doggedly to go in level at the break but Motherwell emerged as 4-0 winners thanks to goals from Wilson Humphries, Johnny Aitkenhead (2) and Archie Kelly.

WEDNESDAY 23RD FEBRUARY 1983

As part of local car dealer Ian Skelly's increasing involvement with the club, a football chat night was held at his showroom. Over 400 people were in attendance to hear words of wisdom from Motherwell manager Jock Wallace, reporter James Sanderson and commentator David Francey.

SATURDAY 23RD FEBRUARY 1991

Superstitious fans were delighted that the next round of the Scottish Cup also fell on the corresponding date from 1952. This time Motherwell did the business at the first time of asking when Falkirk were dispatched 4-2 at Fir Park. The Bairns were leading the First Division at the time and proved stern opposition, equalising twice. Super sub Steve Kirk came off the bench to grab the winner once more with the other goals being provided by Nick Cusack (2) and Joe McLeod.

SUNDAY 24TH FEBRUARY 1963

Brian Martin was born in Bellshill on this date. For years Bellshill boasted the major maternity hospital in Lanarkshire, meaning a huge number of future footballers entered the world within its walls. Martin quickly showed himself to be a classy defender and Tommy McLean paid St Mirren £175,000 for his services in 1991. Martin continued to develop and showed some breath taking form as the club finished third and second in the league in future seasons. He played twice for Scotland as the national team drew 0-0 with Japan and defeated Ecuador 2-1 to finish second in the Kirin Cup of 1995.

SATURDAY 24TH FEBRUARY 1990

After beating Clyde 7-0 in the previous round, a massive Motherwell support gathered on the uncovered Gorgie Road terrace at Tynecastle to watch the side face Hearts in the next round. Unfortunately, it would be a day to remember for all the wrong reasons; a monsoon ensured everyone in the crowd went home soaked to the skin while the players didn't fare much better, losing 4-0. Two goals from John Robertson and one by John Colquhoun had the Jambos on easy street in the first half before Scott Crabbe added another later on.

FRIDAY 24TH FEBRUARY 1995

Alex McLeish swooped to sign Eddie May from Falkirk in a dramatic swap deal. Cup-winning legend Steve Kirk and Paul McGrillen moved to Brockville along with a cheque for £100,000. Eddie May was not a resounding success at Motherwell but he would probably be remembered with a lot more fondness had it not been for the high price paid to secure his signature. Kirk may have struggled to find a starting place in the team towards the end of his spell at Fir Park but he was always good for a goal, as he proved by scoring twice against Motherwell in games to come later in the season.

SATURDAY 25TH FEBRUARY 1978

There was controversy at Fir Park when Rangers picked up a vital two points in their title challenge with a 5-3 win. Motherwell were in control of the game through goals from Jimmy O'Rourke and Vic Davidson when a large part of the visiting support invaded the park. The players were taken off while the crowd was dispersed before revitalised Rangers took advantage of a rattled Mothewell side. Despite a protest the result stood and Rangers eventually won the league – by two points – while Motherwell finished in mid-table.

WEDNESDAY 25TH FEBRUARY 1998

Harri Kampman watched from the stand as his new charges defeated St Johnstone 2-1 at Fir Park. Two goals from Tommy Coyne secured the victory although the closing stages were nervous as the Saints tried to complete their comeback.

MONDAY 25TH FEBRUARY 2008

John Boyle resumed the role of chairman at the club's 102nd AGM. Boyle had stepped down while the club was in administration in 2003 but remained the majority shareholder as efforts to sell up proved futile. It was also announced that the board would look into the feasibility of moving to a new ground away from Fir Park.

SATURDAY 26TH FEBRUARY 1977

The difference between the sides in this cup tie between Motherwell and St Mirren was stark; the hosts were experienced and the guests were youthful and skilful. The 'Well side of this season could be described as physical in their approach and claimed a battling 2-1 win in front of a packed crowd of 27,000, much to the disgust of Buddies manager Alex Ferguson.

SATURDAY 26TH FEBRUARY 2000

Every fan knows Motherwell have a great ability to shoot themselves in the foot at crucial moments and this was one of them. The side knew lower league Partick Thistle were waiting in the quarter-finals but Ayr United left Fir Park with a sensational 4-3 fourth round Scottish Cup victory.

FIR PARK

SATURDAY 27TH FEBRUARY 1937

The Scottish Cup trip to Duns was postponed due to a blizzard. The severity of the weather was put into perspective by the fact that one supporters' coach was marooned by large snow drifts outside Peebles, forcing the fans to spend the night on the bus! Motherwell defeated the Borders side 5-2 when the game was finally played eleven days later at Hawthorn Park.

MONDAY 27TH FEBRUARY 1978

Roger Hynd had won the Manager of the Month award and with it a large bottle of whisky. Before the cup tie at home to Queen's Park he sent the players out with plastic cups filled from the bottle to give the fans a wee dram. Sadly Queen's were not in celebratory mood and ruined the party by winning 3-1.

SUNDAY 27TH FEBRUARY 2000

Midfielder Ged Brannan flew off to start his international career with the Cayman Islands. The tiny association was hoping to exploit a passport loophole to fill its side with experienced British professionals but FIFA quickly put a stop to their plans. Brannan played in only one game, an unofficial friendly with [Washington] DC United, which was lost 5-0.

MONDAY 28TH FEBRUARY 1921

The minutes of a Motherwell board meeting noted the receipt of a letter from the SFA. Clubs were requested to refuse admission to spectators carrying flags or bugles while known delinquents should also be prevented from entering the ground.

WEDNESDAY 29TH FEBRUARY 1956

Fir Park's floodlights were inaugurated with a visit from Preston North End. The English guests were a class apart from the hosts and the legendary Tom Finney scored the winning goal in a 3-2 success. The first Motherwell scorer under the lights was Stuart Brown, with the other strike being generously provided by a Preston own goal. Installing the lights contributed to the club making a loss of £3,657, the first deficit in six years.

MOTHERWELL FC
On This Day

MARCH

WEDNESDAY 1st MARCH 1961

One of the most wonderful Motherwell wins took place at Ibrox on this date. The side had earned a Scottish Cup replay by coming back from two goals down at Fir Park but few gave them a real chance in Glasgow. A sell-out crowd of nearly 90,000 saw Rangers go 2-1 in front but they had no idea what was to come. Pat Delaney equalised with a free-kick before Bobby Roberts poked home on the hour mark to give 'Well the lead. Further goals from Ian St John and Roberts gave a famous 5-2 victory which is still sung about to this day.

WEDNESDAY 1st MARCH 1972

A miners' strike forced the creation of the three-day week as industrial problems ravaged the country. It was decided not to use floodlights, so the cup replay with Ayr took place on a Wednesday afternoon. However, 11,000 people still watched Motherwell progress 2-1.

TUESDAY 1st MARCH 1994

Motherwell failed to take the second 'crack at the cherry' provided by John Philliben's last-gasp cup equaliser at Tannadice. A bumper crowd of over 13,000 squeezed into Fir Park but eventual cup winners Dundee United scored the only goal through Brian Welsh.

SATURDAY 2nd MARCH 1907

The first ever win over Rangers came after seven attempts when Andy Donaldson's goal was enough to secure victory at Fir Park. The match was watched by a crowd of only 4,500.

FRIDAY 2nd MARCH 2001

Two products of the youth system, Stephen McMillan and Lee McCulloch, moved south to join Wigan Athletic in the Second Division for a combined fee of £1.4m. The JJB side were in the middle of an ambitious spending programme which would eventually see them promoted to the English Premiership. McCulloch progressed through two leagues and played at the top level in England before joining Rangers but McMillan's career was ended prematurely by injury.

SATURDAY 3RD MARCH 1956

Pat Quinn made his competitive debut in the loss against Kilmarnock. Quinn had been signed from Bridgeton Waverly and became a key part of Bobby Ancell's midfield. Caps for Scotland and the Scottish League followed but his transfer to Blackpool infuriated the fans as the Ancell Babes began to disperse without ever winning the silverware their flowing football deserved.

WEDNESDAY 3RD MARCH 1971

The sensational Texaco Cup run came to an end in the second leg of the semi-final. Stoke City and Tottenham Hotspur had been defeated and a first-leg draw at Tynecastle was viewed as a good result. But, in front of over 25,000 – a larger crowd than watched Spurs – the job couldn't be finished at Fir Park. Despite a Brian Heron goal, Donald Ford scrambled a last-minute winner as Hearts progressed 3-2 on aggregate to face Wolves in the first ever final of the competition.

WEDNESDAY 4TH MARCH 1931

After several seasons on the fringe of a real title challenge, there was a strong feeling that 1931 could be the triumphant year. The side were leading the race until March when a disastrous 4-1 defeat to Celtic in Glasgow allowed Rangers to move to the top of the table by taking advantage elsewhere. The players were fighting on two fronts which resulted in a cup final appearance – sadly both attempts fell short as the side finished third and lost to Celtic at Hampden Park. Some consolation was that with 102 goals in 38 games, Motherwell finished the season as the division's top scorers.

SATURDAY 4TH MARCH 1939

Celtic were the visitors at Fir Park for the first ever all-ticket game. The Scottish Cup quarter-final attracted a huge crowd of 31,000 who saw Motherwell go 2-0 up before Celtic pulled one back. A clever goal by George Stevenson ensured the hosts would reach Hampden to face Aberdeen in the semi-final.

SATURDAY 5TH MARCH 1910

Winger George Robertson became the first Motherwell player to represent Scotland, in a match against Wales. The game was played at Kilmarnock's Rugby Park in front of a 22,000 crowd and Scotland won the British International Championship match 1-0.

SATURDAY 5TH MARCH 1932

Motherwell and Rangers were fighting it out for the league title but they also met at Ibrox in the Scottish Cup quarter-final. A subdued performance from the Steelmen allowed the hosts to progress 2-0 and a great chance to win the cup was missed – the other semi-finalists finished the league in positions 9, 10 and 14, respectively. But, crucially, Rangers continued involvement in the knock-out competition caused a backlog of league fixtures, allowing Motherwell to open up a significant gap in the championship race. While the loss in the cup cost the club the chance of a historic double, it arguably helped ensure the league flag finally went to Fir Park.

FRIDAY 5TH MARCH 1999

Striker Owen Coyle signed for Dunfermline Athletic after finalising the details of his £170,000 transfer. The move was controversial as it came the day before a Scottish Cup quarter-final with St Johnstone, which Motherwell would go on to lose 2-0, scarcely registering a shot at goal in the 90 minutes. Coyle later said in the media he had been forced out by a member of the Fir Park backroom staff.

MONDAY 5TH MARCH 2001

Record signing John Spencer left the club, the day after his last game in claret and amber. Spencer's move to the Colorado Rapids in the American league had been previously agreed as the club desperately tried to slash the crippling wage bill. By this point it was clear John Boyle's ambitious plans to make Motherwell the third force in Scottish football had failed and major financial restructuring would soon be required. Spenny's last game was a draw – 1-1 – away to Hibs.

IN 1910 GEORGE ROBERTSON WAS THE FIRST 'WELL PLAYER TO REPRESENT SCOTLAND

SATURDAY 6th MARCH 2004

While Motherwell were busy in the league securing a first ever appearance in the post-split top six, the Scottish Cup was also proving successful. The basis of the side's good form was a wonderful run at home from January which saw Dundee United, Dundee, Queen of the South, Kilmarnock, Aberdeen and Partick Thistle beaten in consecutive games. Sadly, the spell came undone at home to Inverness in the cup quarter-final as the First Division team scored early, and were then rarely troubled defensively in their 1-0 win.

SATURDAY 7th MARCH 1959

The title challenge stayed alive into the spring but was soon ended as a disastrous losing run forced the team out of championship contention. The nadir was a heavy defeat to Raith Rovers at Stark's Park, but four wins in the last five ensured the side finished third.

SATURDAY 7th MARCH 1981

Another quarter-final turned out badly when the team travelled to Tannadice in 1981. Dundee United were in their glory days under the tyrannical Jim McLean while Motherwell, though improving, were stuck in the First Division. The visitors eventually lost 6-1 but the home manager still fined his players for failing to entertain the crowd!

SATURDAY 8th MARCH 1952

The successful Scottish Cup run of 1952 almost came unstuck at Ibrox. The hosts had raced into an early lead but despite Motherwell pressure for most of the game no goal appeared to be forthcoming. The breakthrough was finally made with just three minutes remaining when good work by Johnny Aitkenhead, beating two men, set up Tommy Sloan to equalise.

SATURDAY 8th MARCH 1975

Bobby Graham scored the only goal of the cup quarter-final in an incredibly rare triumph at Pittodrie. Motherwell recorded cup wins in the Granite City in 1975 and 1991 but they were isolated successes as the league produced a 28-year victory drought between 1966 and 1994.

SATURDAY 9TH MARCH 1889

Motherwell originally played at Roman Road, the home of Alpha, but decided to search for a new ground. Dalziel Park was opened when Rangers played out a 3-3 exhibition draw but the park was small, muddy and before long another solution would be required.

SATURDAY 9TH MARCH 1957

Bobby Ancell's side were in a great position to challenge for the title but things went pear-shaped after a visit to Ibrox. They were stuffed 5-2 and this sparked a massive eight-game losing run which eventually saw the team finish in seventh place, a bitter disappointment given the earlier situation.

SATURDAY 10TH MARCH 1923

After seeing off Bo'ness in the quarter-final, Motherwell ran out at Hampden Park against Celtic for their first ever Scottish Cup semi-final. Nine special trains were put on to shuttle fans from the town to Glasgow and they were part of a bumper 70,000 crowd. The cup dream took an early blow when a defensive slip allowed Celtic to open the scoring. Several chances were created but a deflected second and some resolute defending by Celtic saw the big day end in defeat.

WEDNESDAY 10TH MARCH 1965

Manager Bobby Ancell had decided to move on to Dundee and the board decided not to stand in his way. Bobby Howitt of Morton was offered the job and accepted – it was anticipated he would take over in April after securing his release from the Greenock club.

SATURDAY 11TH MARCH 1961

After the sensational win at Ibrox in the previous round, there were high hopes that the Scottish Cup could make a return to Fir Park. The visit of local rivals Airdrie proved to be a massive disappointment as high scoring Motherwell were repelled by an inspired display from goalkeeper Leslie. The Diamonds grabbed an undeserved winner against the run of play to set up a semi-final date with Celtic.

SATURDAY 12TH MARCH 1932

Motherwell needed to put the recent Scottish Cup defeat at Ibrox out of their heads and concentrate on the league. Thankfully, this was achieved in great style with a 4-2 win bringing two points at Celtic. The fourth was scored by Willie McFadyen – his 49th league strike of the season, equalling the record held by Jimmy McGrory of Celtic. As Motherwell chased the championship, McFadyen would raise the bar further.

WEDNESDAY 12TH MARCH 1952

Rangers visited Fir Park for the Scottish Cup quarter-final replay. Again, Rangers led but Motherwell equalised early in the second half, the winner following with only ten minutes remaining. A remarkable 35,632 paid to get into the game, a number which stands as Motherwell's record attendance to date. However, as season ticket holders were not counted at the time, the true figure was probably over 37,000.

SATURDAY 12TH MARCH 1966

John 'Dixie' Deans made his debut against Kilmarnock. That game failed to provide a goal but he was soon finding the net with regularity, striking 78 times in 152 league matches. Sadly, red cards also flowed and he was transferred cheaply to Celtic in 1971. There, he won every domestic honour but missed a penalty in the European Cup semi-final shoot-out with Inter Milan.

WEDNESDAY 13TH MARCH 1929

A record crowd of 34,000 was set in 1929 when Celtic arrived for a quarter-final replay. Despite Motherwell leading early on through Bobby Ferrier's goal, they fought back and the prolific Jimmy McGrory got the winner with four minutes remaining.

SATURDAY 13TH MARCH 1965

The confused managerial situation seemed to hurt the team as they went down 2-0 against Kilmarnock. Bobby Ancell was still in charge but it was known he was going to Dundee while replacement Bobby Howitt would soon arrive from Morton. It was far from ideal preparation for a forthcoming cup semi-final with Celtic.

SATURDAY 14TH MARCH 1896

Motherwell were well beaten 6-3 at home to Airdrie as the local rivals continued their early period of Lanarkshire dominance. Motherwell eventually finished eighth out of ten in the Second Division but successfully applied for re-election along with Linthouse and Morton. This was the first of three re-elections as the side struggled to adapt to the national level.

SATURDAY 14TH MARCH 1931

Eight years after the first semi-final, Motherwell once again made it to the last four of the Scottish Cup. This time the venue was Ibrox, the opposition St Mirren and the result more satisfactory as George Stevenson headed the only goal in a 1-0 win. Celtic would be up next in the final.

SATURDAY 14TH MARCH 1964

John Philliben was born on this day in 1964. The defender scored in Scotland's only ever official triumph, the European U19 Championship in 1982. Tommy McLean signed him from Doncaster in 1986 and though not always in the side, he earned the affection of the fans. Sadly he suffered some cruel blows in his time at Motherwell – notably a semi-final penalty miss against Celtic, and not being selected for the 1991 cup final squad.

WEDNESDAY 14TH MARCH 1973

Bobby Howitt tendered his resignation after losing 2-0 at Norwich City in the Texaco Cup. Almost seven years to the day after he stepped into the manger's office, Howitt admitted defeat, having failed to match the relative success of the side before he took over. Howitt agreed to stay until a successor could be found.

SATURDAY 14TH MARCH 1998

The side has delivered a lot of *Schadenfreude* over the years, none more so than when they beat Rangers 2-1 in 1998. Rangers were going for a record tenth league title in a row but came unstuck at Fir Park. There were chances at either end before Willie Falconer won the game with a late diving header.

MONDAY 15TH MARCH 1976

An epic cup tie with Hibs was finally settled at the third time of asking at neutral Ibrox. Games at Fir Park and Easter Road, with extra time, could not produce a winner so another match was played in Glasgow. Peter Marinello and Ian Taylor clinched a 2-1 win despite the SFA declining manager Willie McLean's bid to have the game postponed due to a flu bug sweeping Fir Park.

FRIDAY 15TH MARCH 1996

Tommy Coyne was called up to the Republic of Ireland squad to take on Russia in a friendly. The side would lose 2-0 but Coyne maintained a healthy international career while at Fir Park, at one point overtaking George Stevenson as the club's most capped player before being leapfrogged by Finn Simo Valakari. Coyne also has the distinction of being the first, and to date only, Motherwell player to take part in the World Cup finals.

SATURDAY 16TH MARCH 1949

Goalkeeper John Johnston had a mixed day at Easter Road as he saved two penalties – but sadly the side were already trailing Hibs 5-1 at the time! Johnston's efforts throughout the game kept the last trace of dignity on the scoreline.

MONDAY 16TH MARCH 1959

Pat Holton moved to Chelsea when he was transferred for a fee of £5,000. However, his time at Stamford Bridge was not happy and he played just once before going to Southend United, St Johnstone and finally returning to Hamilton.

SATURDAY 16TH MARCH 1991

After seeing off title-challenging Aberdeen and promotion-chasing Falkirk in earlier rounds, few people expected lowly Morton to pose many problems in the Fir Park quarter-final. However, the Ton produced a stuffy display to limit Motherwell to very few chances throughout the 90 minutes. Dougie Arnott forced David Wylie into a good save but when Ferguson blazed high over the bar Morton had done enough to secure their 0-0 draw.

NO MATTER WHAT METHOD HAS BEEN USED TO PROTECT THE PITCH RECENTLY, WEATHER PROBLEMS HAVE BLIGHTED FIR PARK

SATURDAY 17TH MARCH 1984

With relegation all but confirmed, manager Bobby Watson threw kids into the side in a failed attempt to spark a change of fortune. It did give them some experience but few will want to remember the 6-0 defeat at home to Celtic in the cup.

TUESDAY 17TH MARCH 1987

Over 15,000 watched Motherwell shoot themselves in the foot in a quarter-final replay against Hearts. John Gardiner's mistake at a cross let John Colquhoun grab the only goal. The loss was particularly bitter following the earlier elimination of both halves of the Old Firm.

WEDNESDAY 17TH MARCH 2004

A major obstacle was overcome on the path out of administration when the creditors agreed a repayment package of 20 pence in the pound. Administrator Bryan Jackson noted that several other clubs in this position had not been able to return any of the money due to creditors.

SATURDAY 18TH MARCH 1933

Motherwell maintained their pursuit of the league and cup double with a semi-final win over Clyde at Hampden. Despite the second half being delayed as goalkeeper Alan McClory complained the goal line wasn't straight, goals by Willie McFadyen and Bobby Ferrier won the day.

SATURDAY 19TH MARCH 1898

The SFA decided to award the new ground of Fir Park its only full international in 1898 against Wales. The stadium capacity was raised to 15,000; a record crowd of 7,000 watched Scotland win 5-2.

WEDNESDAY 19TH MARCH 1991

A blustery night in Greenock was the setting for more cup drama in 1991. 'Well old boy John Gahagan equalised Tom Boyd's fortuitous opener and despite strong Motherwell pressure in extra time the game went to penalties. Davie Cooper, Iain Ferguson, Bobby Russell and Steve Kirk all scored while Mark Pickering missed for Morton. Colin O'Neil had the chance to take Motherwell to Hampden with the final penalty and he duly rattled the ball home before celebrating wildly.

SATURDAY 20TH MARCH 1993

Some improved form had dragged Motherwell back from the brink of relegation but there was still a lot to be done to secure the team's top-flight status. The cause was not helped when Partick Thistle won 3-2 at Fir Park despite trailing to goals from Steve Kirk and Paul McGrillen at half-time.

SUNDAY 20TH MARCH 2005

Motherwell's first final in 14 years ended in disaster as Rangers cruised to a 5-1 win. A poor goalkeeping performance from Gordon Marshall did not help, but in truth no one played well and there were few complaints about the heavy loss. David Partridge headed in what turned out to be no more than a consolation goal.

SUNDAY 21ST MARCH 1925

Relegation was a distinct possibility when Motherwell took on Third Lanark in the penultimate game of the season. The sides were at the wrong end of the table and both would eventually finish level on points along with Ayr. Motherwell defeated Thirds but it was the sizable 8-0 result which proved crucial as the 'Well finished ahead of their opponents and Ayr on goal average.

SATURDAY 21ST MARCH 1998

Fresh from the win against Rangers, Motherwell travelled to Easter Road knowing even a draw would all but guarantee SPL football as they had a nine-point gap over Hibs at the bottom. Alex McLeish's men continued to fight for everything and Kevin Harper volleyed home the only goal. Motherwell hit the bar, but the defeat narrowed the gap to six points and gave everyone at Fir Park cause for concern.

TUESDAY 21ST MARCH 2000

If there was any doubt that the era of glamour midweek friendlies was over, then it was proven by this match with IFK Gothenburg. Despite decent opposition and cheap prices, only a small crowd turned up to watch one of the most boring 0-0 draws ever witnessed at Fir Park.

SATURDAY 22ND MARCH 2003

Motherwell reached a semi-final for the first time in 12 years when Stranraer were seen off at Stair Park. An own goal in the first half gave the visitors the lead before the relegation-threatened side strolled home in the second period. After the game, supporters' buses had a food stop in Girvan and as fans queued in the streets waiting to enter the chip shops, the players coach drove through to a heroes' reception.

SATURDAY 23RD MARCH 1889

In the days before bylines, the Chatterer was a frequent commentator on the side's fortunes in the *Motherwell Times*. In his column on March 23, he called for the barricades behind the goals to be tarred to help the players see the posts.

THURSDAY 23RD MARCH 1995

Former Motherwell player Davie Cooper died aged 39. The winger suffered a brain haemorrhage the previous day while recording a coaching film. Cooper had an infectious love for the game and had played in a competitive game for Clydebank at Hearts only a few weeks earlier. Motherwell were in the process of redeveloping the north end of the ground and soon decided the new structure would be known as the Davie Cooper Stand in response to the emotional tributes which would quickly emerge at Fir Park.

SATURDAY 24TH MARCH 1934

There can be few more pleasurable feelings than a convincing derby win but a victory to keep your own title challenge alive and all but relegate the opposition is particularly sweet. That scenario was enjoyed by Motherwell in a 6-3 win at Broomfield in 1964.

TUESDAY 24TH MARCH 1964

Tommy Coakley signed on this day and made his debut shortly after aged only 16. It is believed he is the youngest ever Motherwell player. His nephew, also called Tommy Coakley, failed in an attempt to buy the club from John Boyle over forty years later.

SATURDAY 25TH MARCH 1939

The hunt for the Scottish Cup continued with an Ibrox semi-final against Aberdeen. A crowd of 80,000 saw the Dons take the lead but Davie Mathie's equaliser midway through the second half ensured the sides would soon meet again to settle their differences in a replay.

WEDNESDAY 25TH MARCH 1959

A new era without John 'Sailor' Hunter started at Fir Park, the day after his resignation as secretary had been accepted by the board. Hunter arrived at Fir Park in 1911 and combined managerial duties with the position of secretary for over thirty years. This meant he had almost complete control of the club on a day-to-day basis and not only established the side in the top flight of Scottish football but secured the only league championship, which was won in 1932. He stood down as manager just after the war and passed control of team affairs onto George Stevenson, a player he himself had brought to Fir Park. Both cups were then won with Hunter as club secretary before his failing eyesight finally forced him to retire, aged 80.

SUNDAY 25TH MARCH 2007

An enjoyable evening was spent at Fir Park when the 'greatest ever' awards were announced. The league winning side of 1932 and the cup victors of 1952 were honoured along with Steve Kirk (cult hero), Colin O'Neil (best goal), Tommy McLean (best manager) and Tom Boyd (best captain). The fans' votes for best team produced a slightly bizarre line-up but contained: goalkeeper Ally Maxwell, right-back Davie Whiteford, left-back Joe Wark, right-half Charlie Aitken, centre-half Andy Paton, left-half Bert McCann, wingers John Gahagan and Davie Cooper, and forwards Dougie Arnott, Ian St John, and Willie Pettigrew. The top award of 'greatest ever player' went to Andy Paton, an acknowledgement of his 16 years' service which brought him both domestic cups, a Second Division title and three Scotland caps.

MONDAY 26TH MARCH 1979

Motherwell were in the middle of an eleven-game winless run when they visited Pittodrie and Aberdeen were only too happy to pile on the pain. The teams had recently drawn 1-1 but this time the Dons showed no mercy as they racked up a frightful 8-0 win. This remains Motherwell's record loss.

SATURDAY 27TH MARCH 1926

Bobby Ferrier was made captain for the day and allowed to keep the proceeds from Celtic's visit to Fir Park. The reward served both as a benefit for his previous years of good service and also a sweetener to ensure he stayed for many more to come! This was the first testimonial game played by Motherwell and the side did not let down the star – despite losing a late goal, earlier strikes from Dick Little and Tom Tennant provided a victory more convincing than the 2-1 scoreline suggested.

SATURDAY 27TH MARCH 1954

As Motherwell marched through the Second Division, success also followed in the Scottish Cup. The semi-final against Celtic was a topsy-turvy affair with Motherwell taking the lead and being pegged back within 60 seconds. Celtic then went in front but Charlie Aitken, who missed out on the cup wins due to national service, headed an equaliser. Motherwell almost won the tie late on, but Sloan fired over the bar.

SATURDAY 27TH MARCH 1965

Bobby Ancell was in charge for the last time, although new manager Howitt gave advice, for the cup semi-final with Celtic. Despite leading twice through Joe McBride, the game was drawn 2-2.

TUESDAY 27TH MARCH 1990

Tommy Boyd made his first start for Scotland at senior level when a B side took on Yugoslavia at Fir Park. The match ended in a scoreless draw but boss Andy Roxburgh was pleased with what he saw from the young full-back. Boyd went on to win 72 full caps for his country.

THE ANCELL BABES THRILLED THE FANS WITH THEIR PLAY BUT CAME UP SHORT OF SILVERWARE

FRIDAY 28th MARCH 2003

A national newspaper carried the story that the 10 players made redundant when the club entered administration were continuing their attempt to be paid in full, rather than receive the same percentage as everyone else. The players, backed by the Scottish Professional Footballers' Association, had been granted an appeal by the SPL. However, legally the players had little claim to the extra money and even the Inland Revenue eventually waived its right to be treated as a preferential creditor to allow everyone a share of the pot.

WEDNESDAY 29th MARCH 1939

Motherwell made no mistake against Aberdeen at the second time of asking with a convincing semi-final replay win. Goals from Davie Mathie, John McCulloch and Hutton Bremner secured a comfortable 3-1 win to set up a final clash with Clyde.

SATURDAY 29th MARCH 1947

A marathon Scottish Cup semi-final with Hibs ended in disappointment. Motherwell trailed to a goal from Eddie Turnbull but Willie Kilmarnock equalised and the side pressed strongly for the winner. No further breakthrough was made before the end of 90 minutes and, with the tie being finished on the day, another 52 minutes were played before the decisive goal arrived. Sadly it was a fluke for Hibs, when Hugh Howie met John Johnston's clearance and sent it into the net from sixty yards. The board sent a letter to the players congratulating them on their performance but this would have been scant consolation compared to a cup final appearance.

SATURDAY 29th MARCH 1952

By 1952 it had been decided that replays should once more be used to settle Scottish Cup semi-finals and that set the scene for another mammoth tie with Hearts. The Jambos took an early lead through Conn but Willie Watters did enough to secure a replay when he equalised via the post in the second half. A huge crowd of 98,547 crammed the Hampden Park terraces to watch the game.

WEDNESDAY 30TH MARCH 1977

Motherwell recorded an unremarkable 0-0 draw at Partick Thistle but enormous credit went to keeper Stuart Rennie who emerged for the second half to play despite suffering a broken finger. It was later plastered at Glasgow Royal Infirmary. Rennie had form for bravery, though, as he had previously played on in a game after having six stitches inserted in a face wound at the half-time break. Rennie was one of the best goalkeepers Motherwell have had and made 174 league appearances in his time at Fir Park after arriving from Falkirk in 1973 as part of the deal which took Kirkie Lawson to Brockville.

SATURDAY 30TH MARCH 1991

Just four days before the cup semi-final with Celtic, the sides met in Glasgow at Parkhead. It was the visitors who recorded a confidence boosting win thanks to goals from Tom Boyd and Iain Ferguson countering the opener from then Celt Tommy Coyne. This was the last league game of the season between the clubs and with Motherwell having an excellent record of two wins, one draw and just one defeat, hopes were high for the trip to Hampden Park. However, Celtic would still be favourites as Motherwell had not beaten them in the cup at the home of Scottish football in all seven earlier attempts.

SATURDAY 30TH MARCH 1996

The Motherwell Supporters' Association celebrated their 50th anniversary with a dinner dance in the Davie Cooper suite. The association had been formed in 1946.

TUESDAY 30TH MARCH 1999

Scotland under-21s lined up at Fir Park when they took on the Czech Republic. Some local interest was provided by striker Lee McCulloch who played from the start before being substituted in the second half. McCulloch struggled to make the breakthrough into the full team but eventually established himself on the wing in the Euro 2008 qualifying campaign, contributing a goal in the home win over the Ukraine.

SATURDAY 31st MARCH 1934

Over the years, March 31 has been a largely disappointing day in the history of Motherwell. It started to go wrong as early as 1934 when St Mirren gained revenge for their semi-final defeat of 1931 by beating Motherwell 3-1 at Hampden Park.

SATURDAY 31st MARCH 1951

A rare bright spot on this day occurred in 1951 when Motherwell defeated Hibs in the cup semi-final. Goals from Archie Kelly (2) and Donald McLeod kept the cup double dream alive in a 3-2 win.

SATURDAY 31st MARCH 1962

Motherwell were dealt a blow when Bert McCann was badly injured in the first-half of the semi-final with Rangers. They took advantage with two strikes before the break and though Bobby Roberts would reply, a third goal clinched victory late on.

WEDNESDAY 31st MARCH 1965

Motherwell would frequently come undone against Celtic and this semi-final replay was a fine example of that. Missing Willie Hunter due to injury, there was no sign of the side which caused problems in the original tie and little credit could be taken from the 3-0 loss which was Bobby Howitt's first game in charge.

WEDNESDAY 31st MARCH 1976

The most devastating of the many semi-final defeats on this day came in 1976. Playing in a white strip with claret and amber stripes, Motherwell were two up at half-time thanks to Stewart McLaren and Willie Pettigrew. The referee, JPR Gordon, then took a decisive role by awarding a penalty for a 'trip' on Derek Johnstone, and ignoring a blatant foul in the box on Pettigrew. Rangers eventually won 3-2 although few eyebrows were raised when Gordon was later banned for accepting gifts before a European game.

SATURDAY 31st MARCH 1984

The misery on this day was not just consigned to the cup. A 3-0 defeat at Ibrox, in front of less than 9,000, guaranteed relegation to the First Division.

MOTHERWELL FC
On This Day

APRIL

SATURDAY 1st APRIL 2000

Billy Davies had assembled an expensive side but the rewards were seen on the park. The team were challenging for Europe along with Hearts and recorded a vital win at home to St Johnstone with two late goals. The visitors seemed set to leave with the points but Brannan levelled from the spot before Martyn Corrigan's drive was fumbled into the corner of the net. The full-back rarely found himself on the scoresheet but this was a vital strike.

THURSDAY 1st APRIL 2004

Veteran striker Gerry Britton was signed by Terry Butcher to add depth to the squad for the closing weeks of the 2003/04 season. Britton was not an especially popular addition in the eyes of the Motherwell fans but, though his appearances were limited, his enthusiasm won over the crowd before he was released at the end of the year.

THURSDAY 2nd APRIL 1998

The funeral of Andy Russell took place at Daldowie Crematorium on this day in 1998. While players come and go, Andy had been the groundsman at Fir Park for the better part of forty years. He and his Alsatian, Tizer, guarded the grass ferociously from straying feet.

WEDNESDAY 3rd APRIL 1974

Fog caused the abandonment of a game between Hibs and Motherwell at Easter Road after only 18 minutes. There had been an exciting start to the match, with Cropley scoring a penalty for Hibs and Willie Watson missing a similar award for Motherwell.

WEDNESDAY 3rd APRIL 1991

Motherwell took on Celtic at Hampden for the right to face Dundee United in the Scottish Cup final. Celtic were dominant for the majority of the game but it was Motherwell who went closest to a goal. A strong penalty claim by Arnott was not given, then Iain Ferguson rattled the post with a thirty-yard free-kick in the dying minutes. The goalless draw forced a replay.

WEDNESDAY 4TH APRIL 1962

Motherwell lost at home to continental opposition for the first time when French champions Nimes won at Fir Park. Sandy Jones got the goal for Motherwell in a 2-1 defeat. The match was played as part of a hectic run of four games in eight days with Rangers (cup), Hearts and Falkirk (both league), being the other opponents.

MONDAY 5TH APRIL 1954

The side paid a high price for failing to beat Celtic at the first attempt when the Glasgow giants won the replay 3-1. Hunter got the consolation for Motherwell as yet another trip to Hampden Park ended in disappointment. Celtic, who would go on to beat Aberdeen in the final, had now ended Motherwell hopes at Hampden on five occasions and this misery would be repeated several times in the future.

SATURDAY 5TH APRIL 1958

A disastrous start which saw Clyde race into a 3-0 lead in this Hampden semi-final couldn't quite be overturned. A hat-trick from Coyle put the Bully Wee in a dominant position before Pat Quinn and Ian St John set up an exciting finish. Clyde were only guaranteed their passage to the final when a last gasp header by Willie McSeveney rebounded to safety having struck the underside of the bar as Motherwell looked to equalise.

SUNDAY 5TH APRIL 1959

The Supporters' Association chose Ian St John as Player of the Year for this season. The ballot was a tight affair, with Pat Quinn and John Martis both close in pursuit, but St John's 24 league goals, plus eight more in the two cups, were enough to give him the prestigious honour.

SATURDAY 5TH APRIL 1975

Motherwell were on course for a semi-final win over Lanarkshire rivals Airdrie thanks to a second-half goal from Willie Pettigrew. However, disaster struck with only ten minutes remaining when an own goal by Stewart McLaren gave the Diamonds an undeserved replay.

SUNDAY 6TH APRIL 1879

John 'Sailor' Hunter was born in Paisley in 1879. His footballing career started with Abercorn before he moved to Liverpool, helping the Merseyside club to win their first ever league title. He played for Hearts, Woolwich Arsenal and Portsmouth before going to Dundee where he scored the winning goal in their only Scottish Cup final win in 1910. He then signed for Clyde but retired through injury without making an appearance before joining Motherwell as secretary manager.

MONDAY 7TH APRIL 1952

The semi-final duel with Hearts continued when the sides drew 1-1 in the first replay at Hampden. This time it was Motherwell who took the lead first but Hearts quickly equalised. Despite an additional period of 30 minutes, there was still no winning goal and a third game was required.

WEDNESDAY 7TH APRIL 1954

Motherwell's Division B exile ended after just one season. The title was secured when Arbroath were beaten 2-1 in a nervous game at Fir Park. Willie McSeveney had given the Steelmen the lead but after a second-half equaliser it took a Willie Redpath penalty to secure the points.

WEDNESDAY 7TH APRIL 1976

Willie Pettigrew made his debut for Scotland against Switzerland and scored the only goal of the game after just two minutes. This remains the fastest ever debut goal by a Scotland player. Pettigrew played another four times for his country and his second goal, against Wales, would be the last strike by a Motherwell player in national colours for over thirty years.

SATURDAY 7TH APRIL 1979

After a horrific run of form, the relegation which had long been inevitable was confirmed with a 3-0 defeat at Tynecastle. It would herald the start of three seasons outside the top flight, the only occasion Motherwell have not secured immediate promotion. Several players were allowed to leave as Motherwell began to restructure for the difficult period to come.

SATURDAY 8TH APRIL 1967

The match-day programme offered a chance to win a trip to Wembley for the forthcoming England-Scotland international. It was the famous 3-2 victory for Scotland so no doubt the winners enjoyed their prize!

SATURDAY 8TH APRIL 1978

Pre-match entertainment before the Dundee United match was provided by the Hamilton aero-modelling club and the final of the club's target golf competition.

WEDNESDAY 9TH APRIL 1952

The mammoth battle with Hearts was finally settled at the third attempt. The second replay was goalless at half-time before Archie Kelly and Wilson Humphries put Motherwell in front. Hearts pulled one back but Willie Redpath's last-minute goal sent Motherwell to the final.

SATURDAY 9TH APRIL 1955

Stirling Albion were defeated 3-1 at Fir Park as the side battled to maintain top-flight status. Albion were adrift at the bottom but five other teams fought desperately to avoid the second relegation spot.

WEDNESDAY 9TH APRIL 1975

A sense of injustice at being taken to a replay by Airdrie might have inspired Motherwell but instead both teams were flat in this cup semi-final. Scoring chances were rare before a controversial decision handed Airdrie victory. Goalkeeper Stuart Rennie was penalised for taking more than four steps when carrying the ball – a violation rarely punished – giving John Lapsley the chance to score the winner following an indirect free-kick.

TUESDAY 9TH APRIL 1991

The beast was slain. Celtic, after inflicting endless pain on Motherwell at Hampden, were finally beaten in a semi-final replay. The usual pattern seemed set to continue as Celtic led 2-1 at the break but Dougie Arnott got his second to equalise and with 15 minutes left the game was level. Colin O'Neil's astonishing 35-yard drive found the top corner and when Steve Kirk produced an outrageous lob for the fourth, Motherwell were in their first cup final in 37 years.

SATURDAY 10TH APRIL 1954

Motherwell played in the highest competitive draw recorded in the UK, matching Dumbarton in a 12-goal thriller at Fir Park. Despite left-winger Archie Williams grabbing a hat-trick, the Sons, who would finish last in the Scottish league, performed brilliantly to hold already-promoted Motherwell. The match was truly remarkable as Motherwell were 4-2 down after only 16 minutes but recovered to lead 6-4 by the break! The second half was a distinctly more sedate affair with only two goals coming for the visitors, the second a late equaliser. After the match the players went off to Turnberry for a few days' relaxation as a reward for their efforts.

SATURDAY 11TH APRIL 1931

After years of going close in the league without winning the competition, Motherwell would develop a similar relationship with the Scottish Cup. Perhaps things would have been different if the first final against Celtic had ended in success rather than heartbreak. The cup looked to be going to Lanarkshire as George Stevenson and John McMenemy put the team in front and it stayed that way until the 80th minute when McGrory pulled one back. Even then there was little to worry the Motherwell defence until two minutes from time when a hopeful cross was deflected into his own net by Alan Craig. Craig responded to the shout of "go for it, Alan" which was directed at keeper Alan McClory. As McClory rushed out to collect the ball, the touch from Craig left him helpless and gave Celtic an undeserved second chance.

SATURDAY 12TH APRIL 1969

After relegation in 1968, Motherwell ensured they wouldn't miss out on the top flight for long as a wonderful run after Christmas brought them the Second Division title. Promotion was secured at Boghead when Dumbarton were beaten 4-2. Tom Donnelly, Dixie Deans, Jumbo Muir and John Goldthorp ensured promotion with five games of the season still remaining.

THE TEAM MAY HAVE COME UP SHORT IN THE SCOTTISH CUP BUT WON PROMOTION TO THE TOP FLIGHT (SEE OVER)

SATURDAY 13TH APRIL 1935

Motherwell won 3-0 at Falkirk thanks to goals from Bert Cleland, Willie McFadyen and George Stevenson but two subsequent defeats would leave the side in seventh place. It was the end of the era when Motherwell challenged right at the top of the Scottish game as the previous eight years had been spent in the top three. Despite the occasional title challenge in the years to come, Motherwell (and indeed no other small town team) has since provided such a consistent challenge to the Old Firm.

WEDNESDAY 13TH APRIL 1960

The series of evening friendly matches continued when Athletic Bilbao visited Fir Park. The Basques finished third in La Liga and a crowd of 18,000 braved the torrential rain to watch them. Motherwell raced into a two-goal lead but the guests levelled before the break. However, a goal by Ian St John secured a deserved win.

SATURDAY 13TH APRIL 1985

Motherwell may have been in the First Division but were in high spirits when they travelled to take on Celtic in yet another Hampden semi-final clash. The underdogs took the lead through Gary McAllister and though Junior Burns equalised it was Motherwell who continued to press. A winner looked likely when Graeme Forbes met a cross with a header but his attempt floated just the wrong side of the post and the game ended level.

MONDAY 14TH APRIL 1969

Just days after clinching promotion back to Division One, Motherwell ensured they would go up as champions with a crushing 7-1 victory over Stenhousemuir. Goals from Dixie Deans, John Goldthorp (2), Jumbo Muir (2), Tom Donnelly and Bobby Campbell contributed to the tally of 112 which came at a rate of more than three per game.

SATURDAY 14TH APRIL 1973

After Bobby Howitt's departure, Ian St John returned to his home-town club as manager. His first game brought instant success in a 1-0 win over Hibs at Fir Park.

SATURDAY 15TH APRIL 1916

Football continued through the First World War but at times two games were played on the same day. Motherwell took on Ayr United at Fir Park in a 3.30pm kick-off and lost 3-0 before regrouping for a 6.30pm meeting with Celtic. Things didn't get any better but at least a goal was scored, this time in a 3-1 defeat which ended in near darkness.

WEDNESDAY 15TH APRIL 1931

After the devastating draw with Celtic in the cup final a few days previously, Motherwell tried to go one better and lift the trophy in the replay. Unfortunately, the opponents proved stronger and despite goals from George Stevenson and John Murdoch, Celtic ran out comfortable 4-2 winners.

SATURDAY 15TH APRIL 1933

On the second anniversary of the cup final replay defeat against Celtic, Motherwell returned to try again. The old trophy proved elusive once more and despite having the better of the game the team lost 1-0. Tommy McKenzie and Ben Ellis got in each other's way in attempting to clear and Jimmy McGrory took advantage of the situation to score the only goal. The usually reliable Stevenson missed a late one-on-one with the keeper having gone past three defenders – another chance was gone.

SATURDAY 15TH APRIL 1961

What should be a day of reflective glory for Motherwell was ruined as Scotland were hammered 9-3 by England at Wembley. Bert McCann, Pat Quinn and Ian St John were all selected for the side but they had little to cheer as they were torn apart by the Auld Enemy. It would be over thirty years until three Motherwell players were picked in the same Scotland side again.

MONDAY 15TH APRIL 1996

Wolves provided the opposition for Jim Griffin's testimonial. Griff had come through the Fir Park youth system in 1986 but sadly injury hampered his career and eventually forced his early retirement from the game.

SATURDAY 16th APRIL 1921

Motherwell forward Hugh Ferguson set a new individual league scoring record when he grabbed all four goals in the 4-0 win over Aberdeen. That took his total to 40 for the season and further strikes contributed to a massive 42 for the year. Ferguson remains Motherwell's all-time top scorer with 283.

SATURDAY 16th APRIL 1932

Motherwell had been league leaders for some time and could all but guarantee the title with a win at home to Cowdenbeath. Goals from Bobby Ferrier and John McMenemy had effectively secured the win before attention turned to Willie McFadyen to see if he could break the scoring record for the season. He missed several chances but eventually got his historic 50th when he acrobatically converted a rebound off the bar. Motherwell were not officially champions as a loss in the last game could still allow Rangers to snatch the title on goal average if they won their remaining matches.

WEDNESDAY 16th APRIL 1980

A run of just one defeat in 17 gave Motherwell an outside chance of promotion. However, those hopes were killed off with a 2-0 loss at Clyde. The season ended poorly and Motherwell finished in sixth place, several points behind the promoted teams.

MONDAY 17th APRIL 1967

Chris McCart was born on this day in 1967. After coming through the youth system he played over 250 league games between 1984 and 1997. He also took a winner's medal from the 1991 FA Cup Final and gained both Scotland B and Scottish League caps.

SATURDAY 17th APRIL 1982

After three years in the First Division, Motherwell returned to the big time as they cruised to promotion. That was sealed with a 3-1 win at Falkirk.

WEDNESDAY 17th APRIL 1985

After being given a fright in the first game, Celtic made no mistake against Motherwell in the semi-final replay, progressing with a 3-0 win.

TUESDAY 18TH APRIL 1978

The SFA fined Rangers £2,000 as a result of their fans' invasion of Fir Park earlier in the season. Motherwell had been leading 2-0 when the game was halted and Rangers went on to win 5-3 after order had been restored. The committee had originally recommended that the game be replayed but the Scottish League refused to accept this. Director Ian Livingstone said, "There is no way this penalty is a deterrent".

THURSDAY 18TH APRIL 1996

Paul Lambert was among those nominated for the Scottish Professional Footballers' Association Player of the Year. The honour came despite Motherwell having had a difficult spell with injuries which meant that much of the season was spent at the wrong end of the table. Paul Gascoigne, Andy Goram (both Rangers) and Tom Boyd (Celtic) were the other nominees, with Gascoigne winning the award.

SATURDAY 19TH APRIL 1952

At long last Motherwell finally lifted the Scottish Cup when the side beat Dundee 4-0 at Hampden. A massive crowd of 136,274 saw Motherwell withstand severe pressure in the first half as Willie Kilmarnock played a captain's role by clearing off the line on various occasions. Things changed after the break and goals from Jimmy Watson, Willie Redpath, Wilson Humphries and Archie Kelly ensured claret and amber ribbons would finally be attached to the famous trophy.

WEDNESDAY 19TH APRIL 1978

The club released a statement saying that the chairman, Neil Hepburn, had resigned for personal reasons. Ian Livingstone was appointed to the vacant position with William Samuel serving as the vice chair.

SATURDAY 19TH APRIL 2003

The cup had provided a great distraction to the struggles in the league and the club took part in a sensational semi-final with Rangers at Hampden. Despite going behind within a minute, wonderful goals from Steven Craig and James McFadden gave Motherwell a half-time lead. Rangers were too strong though and recovered to win 4-3.

SATURDAY 20TH APRIL 1963

Motherwell reserve 'keeper Willie Murdoch played in goal for the Scotland amateur side against Wales in Wrexham. The 21-year-old was the first, and to date the only, player to have achieved this honour while playing for Motherwell, as both Bert McCann and Hastie Weir won their amateur caps while still at Queen's Park.

SATURDAY 20TH APRIL 1968

Relegation was confirmed with a 1-0 defeat at home to Clyde. Only 2,000 fans decided to turn up which showed just how desperate the situation had become. Bobby Howitt was struggling to match the previous heroics of Bobby Ancell as manager and after a dismal year which featured a mere six wins in 34 league games, the side could have no complaints about going down.

SATURDAY 20TH APRIL 1985

Tommy McLean tasted success in his first season at Fir Park as he successfully guided the team back to the Premier League. Promotion was achieved with a 1-0 win at Partick Thistle thanks to a goal from John McStay. John was part of the famous McStay footballing family but is best remembered for being the victim of a Duncan Ferguson headbutt when playing for Raith Rovers at Ibrox, an action which resulted in the Rangers striker being sent to prison for assault.

TUESDAY 20TH APRIL 2004

After a long battle, Motherwell emerged from administration on this day in 2004. The Court of Session in Edinburgh approved the club's petition to discharge its administrators and resume trading again as a normal limited company. Bryan Jackson of administrator PKF had been responsible for turning round the club's finances and majority shareholder John Boyle paid tribute to him and his team: "I would like to thank the administrators for the valuable assistance they have given the club. Motherwell is emerging from administration on a sound financial footing and can meet the challenges ahead with confidence."

JOHN BOYLE AND PAT NEVIN IN HAPPIER TIMES

SATURDAY 21st APRIL 1951

Missed chances cost Motherwell the opportunity of a cup double as Celtic won the final at Hampden Park. Archie Kelly, Wilson Humphries and Johnny Aitkenhead might have found the net but didn't, meaning McPhail's solitary goal was enough to win the trophy for the Hoops.

SUNDAY 21st APRIL 2002

A pathetic Motherwell team were taken apart at Easter Road as Hibs gained revenge for their earlier 4-0 defeat. A similar scoreline on this occasion did not flatter the hosts but at least SPL football had already been guaranteed for the next season. This was Eric Black's last game in charge as he resigned when the club went into administration.

SATURDAY 22nd APRIL 1939

Motherwell missed out on the chance to claim a Scottish football record when they lost the cup final 4-0 to Clyde. The Second World War prompted the postponement of the tournament, meaning Clyde held the cup for eight years until competition resumed in 1947.

SATURDAY 23rd APRIL 1932

The dream was finally realised as Rangers stumbled at home to Clyde, guaranteeing Motherwell would be champions of Scotland 1931/32. The Ibrox men needed to win their remaining games and hope Motherwell slipped up at home to Clyde in their only fixture still outstanding. However, the Bully Wee secured a point at Ibrox to hand Motherwell the title without having to kick a ball.

SATURDAY 23rd APRIL 1994

The beautiful football played under Tommy McLean produced some fabulous wins and some great goals, none more so than this 2-0 win at Easter Road. Miodrag Krivokapic, a cult hero with the fans for his calm style, carried the ball out of defence and released Coyne on the right. Mio continued his run forward and met the return cross with a perfect header to leave Jim Leighton helpless. He celebrated his only goal for the club in fantastic fashion by leaping onto the perimeter fencing.

SATURDAY 24TH APRIL 1982

With promotion already in the bag, the only question that remained was whether Motherwell would go up as champions. The title was secured at home against Clydebank with a dire 0-0 draw which was at odds with the high-scoring style that characterised the team throughout the season. The BBC team filming the game might not have been delighted with the dull showing on offer but that made no difference to the fans who piled onto the pitch to celebrate with the players at the full-time whistle.

WEDNESDAY 24TH APRIL 2002

The darkest day in the history of the club was on April 24 2002. John Boyle announced that his plan to make Motherwell the third force in Scottish football had failed and that the club was to be put into administration while he attempted to sell his controlling stake. In effect, being in administration protected the club from its creditors while going into a period of financial restructuring. Bryan Jackson of administrators PKF was appointed by the Court of Session to take over the day-to-day running of the club. Chief executive Pat Nevin resigned in protest at the decision to go into administration while manager Eric Black quit as he felt it was unfair to stay when his promises to players would surely be broken in the spate of redundancies which were inevitable. Nevin claimed that the club could trade its way out of the situation with a further cash injection from John Boyle. Terry Butcher, previously the assistant manager, took charge of team affairs.

TUESDAY 25TH APRIL 1933

Motherwell's reign as champions of Scotland came to an end when the side could only manage a 1-1 draw at Third Lanark. However, by then Motherwell would have needed to win all their remaining games while hoping Rangers slipped up elsewhere if they were to defend their title successfully.

SUNDAY 26th APRIL 1936

Pat Quinn was born in Glasgow on this day in 1936. He became a member of the famous Ancell Babes before moving to Blackpool the year after Ian St John departed. The loss of Quinn after St John was arguably the beginning of the end for the Babes who failed to win a major trophy despite playing superb football for many years.

TUESDAY 26th APRIL 1960

A crowd of 25,000 turned up at Fir Park to watch Brazilians Flamengo turn up to take on Motherwell in a glamour friendly. The guests took an early lead but goals from Willie Hunter and Ian St John put the hosts in front at half-time. What followed after the break was simply remarkable as a sensational performance, including a double hat-trick from St John, produced a 9-2 win.

SATURDAY 26th APRIL 1975

This season saw the end of the old Division One which meant only the top ten teams would be in the top flight at the start of the inaugural Premier League. Motherwell were in a good position and knew that a draw at home to Dumbarton in the last game would be enough to secure tenth, but in the event a convincing 3-1 win was recorded thanks to goals from Bobby Graham, Jimmy Miller and Jim McIlwraith. Motherwell finished in the final qualifying spot, two points above rivals Airdrie.

MONDAY 26th APRIL 1993

The South Stand enjoyed its official opening when Coventry City made the trip north. Motherwell fans were able to use the facility normally reserved for away supporters and saw goals from Ally Graham and Steve Kirk ensure a 2-1 victory.

TUESDAY 26th APRIL 1994

The title challenge was kept alive for a bit longer when Rangers were defeated 2-1 at Fir Park. A wonderful goalkeeping display from Sieb Dykstra, along with goals from John Philliben and Tommy Coyne, gave the hosts victory.

SATURDAY 27TH APRIL 1895

The Lanarkshire Cup was won for the first time in 1895. Special trains ran from Motherwell to Airdrie and fans watched the 'Well beat Albion Rovers 7-3 in the final. A large crowd welcomed the heroes at the Cross on their return to the town before the celebrations progressed to the Brandon Hall. The tournament was once a prominent fixture in the Lanarkshire football calendar but lost its competitive edge over the years before the last cup was won by Airdrie in 1996. Motherwell won the local cup on a record 32 occasions.

MONDAY 27TH APRIL 1953

Motherwell's first ever relegation was confirmed in the worst possible way. Rivals Airdrie defeated Third Lanark 4-2 to move beyond the reach of the Steelmen, meaning Motherwell would line up in Division B for season 1952/53.

SATURDAY 27TH APRIL 2002

A large crowd travelled with Motherwell to Rugby Park to watch the first game after administration had been announced. The players knew they were playing together for the last time but produced an inspired performance to win 4-1. Derek Adams' first-half goal was equalised but James McFadden, Stuart Elliot and Stephen Pearson ensured victory for the visitors. The full impact of administration was realised the following Monday when the players were called into Fir Park to hear their fate. Several were released from their contracts while Mark Brown, Stephen Cosgrove, Andy Dow, Eddie Forrest, Roberto Martinez, Brian MacDonald, Karl Ready and Greg Strong were all made redundant. Three members of the non-playing staff also lost their jobs as the administrator streamlined the club in a bid to survive.

SATURDAY 28TH APRIL 1956

Andy Paton was given a silver cup to mark the award of the Supporters' Association's first Player of the Year at a dinner dance in Overtown Miners' Welfare Institute. Club secretary John Hunter, who had signed Paton in 1942, made the presentation.

SATURDAY 29TH APRIL 1989

Motherwell had done enough to stay clear of the one relegation spot in the Premier League but the season had few memorable moments. One came near the end of the year when 2,703 people watched Steve Kirk destroy St Mirren. All four goals in the 4-0 win came from Kirk's right foot as he finished top scorer for the season with 18.

SATURDAY 30TH APRIL 1927

Cardiff won the FA Cup Final by beating Arsenal. The winning goal was scored by former Motherwell striker Hugh Ferguson as the cup left England for the only time. Ferguson eventually returned to Scotland with Dundee but couldn't settle and eventually committed suicide aged just 32.

SATURDAY 30TH APRIL 1937

Celtic were handed their heaviest ever defeat when they were dismantled at Fir Park. Motherwell were 4-0 up before Celtic suffered injuries to Morrison, who had to go off, and keeper Kennaway who soldiered on. Motherwell showed no sympathy and racked up another four goals without reply to triumph 8-0. Alex Stewart scored six with the others coming from Duncan Ogilvie and George Stevenson.

SATURDAY 30TH APRIL 1955

Just one season after being promoted, Motherwell were in trouble once more. A 3-0 defeat at Ibrox was enough to condemn the side to a finish in the relegation zone, prompting manager George Stevenson to consider his future. However, a planned expansion of the league gave Motherwell a possible lifeline and the fate of the club would be decided in board meetings rather than on the football field.

SATURDAY 30TH APRIL 1994

Motherwell followed up the home win over Rangers with another match at Fir Park against Kilmarnock. The Rugby Parkers were fighting relegation but a win would be enough to guarantee Motherwell third place and European football as a result. The game wasn't spectacular but a typical poacher's goal by Tommy Coyne won the points.

MOTHERWELL FC
On This Day

MAY

SATURDAY 1st MAY 1965

Liverpool won the FA Cup Final 2-1 against Leeds United. The winning goal was scored by ex-Motherwell star Ian St John in the second period of extra time. St John had been a prolific scorer for the 'Well grabbing an astonishing 80 goals in 113 league appearances. His cup-winning strike came almost four years to the day after he had joined the Anfield club for a fee of £37,500.

SATURDAY 2nd MAY 1998

Motherwell led twice against St Johnstone before losing 3-2 but there was still reason to celebrate. Hibs lost at home to Dundee United meaning the Easter Road side, under the stewardship of Alex McLeish, were officially relegated and would be spending the next season in the First Division as 'Well survived.

THURSDAY 2nd MAY 2002

The 'Well Worth Saving' group held its first public meeting in the Davie Cooper Stand to discuss what could be done about the club going into administration. A committee was quickly organised and started to raise funds. A proposal to form a Supporters' Trust was backed by those present.

TUESDAY 3rd MAY 1994

The title dream ended on this day when a rare bad performance from 'keeper Sieb Dykstra allowed Dundee United to leave Fir Park with a 2-1 win. Motherwell could still have matched Rangers' points total had the Ibrox club lost all their games but their vastly superior goal difference meant Motherwell were fighting for second place.

SATURDAY 3rd MAY 2003

Terry Butcher's young side were battling bravely against the drop and faced a six-point clash against relegation rivals Dundee United. In an up and down game Motherwell led then trailed and eventually settled for a point in a 2-2 draw. Motherwell remained last, but only by a point, and with a superior goal difference and a game in hand, there was still hope the team could lift themselves above United.

TUESDAY 4TH MAY 1954

The board decided to make the first material change to Fir Park in some years by building a covered enclosure along the east side of the terracing. Around £6,500 was earmarked for the project but major work would need to be done on the roof after a storm caused damage a few years later.

SATURDAY 4TH MAY 1991

The build up to the cup final continued with a fine win over Rangers at a sunny Fir Park. Rangers led Aberdeen by two points going into the penultimate game of the title race and hoped to clinch the championship. Initially, things went for them as Aberdeen trailed elsewhere but nerves were shaken when John Philliben smashed the opening goal in off the bar. Aberdeen turned things around but despite Rangers' pressure they could not equalise. Mark Walters blazed a penalty high into the north terracing before two breakaway goals from Dougie Arnott wrapped up a 3-0 win. The additional goals late on meant Aberdeen only needed to draw with Rangers on the last day of the season to be champions but instead they lost 2-0 at Ibrox.

MONDAY 5TH MAY 1997

With two games remaining Motherwell were three points adrift in the play-off spot and an unenviable sudden-death showdown with Airdrie was looming large on the horizon. Few gave the team a chance when they travelled to Ibrox against a Rangers side needing a win to secure their record-equalling ninth title in a row on the May Day bank holiday. But a breathtaking performance sliced the champions-elect apart and although Mark Hateley headed against the bar, there were not too many frights as the team defended Owen Coyle's opening goal. Coyle then calmly slotted home a late penalty to make sure of the points and Motherwell would be safe if they could match the result of Hibs on the last day of the season.

THURSDAY 6TH MAY 1886

The first step towards the formation of Motherwell was taken when members of Alpha met and decided to disband their club and reform. Originally, they wished to retain their existing name but develop a new constitution.

SATURDAY 6TH MAY 1989

Long-serving winger Johnny Gahagan was honoured with a testimonial match against a Premier League select. Gahagan had signed for the club in December 1979 and would leave in 1990, narrowly missing out on the Scottish Cup triumph the following year. He did play a prominent role in that run as his goal for Morton took the quarter-final to a penalty shoot-out at Cappielow.

SATURDAY 6TH MAY 1995

European football was all but secured for the second season running when Kilmarnock were defeated 2-0 at Fir Park. The new North Stand, soon named after Davie Cooper, was in use for the first time and goals from Dougie Arnott and Eddie May picked up the points. The runners-up spot was soon secured when Hibs dropped points against Celtic meaning Motherwell had achieved their highest league finish since 1934.

SATURDAY 6TH MAY 2000

A poor run of form gave Hearts the initiative in the race for Europe and Motherwell needed to win their last three games to have a chance of catching them. Two late Kevin Twaddle goals defeated Hibs at Fir Park, but St Johnstone holding Hearts at Tynecastle gave the fight a much needed boost.

SATURDAY 6TH MAY 2006

A distinctly average 1-1 draw with Dundee United signalled the end of the Terry Butcher era at Fir Park. Butcher had been appointed as manager in the aftermath of administration in 2002 and although relegation was only escaped on a technicality in his first season, he soon went from strength to strength. After securing two top-six finishes and a cup final, he decided to move on to new challenges in Sydney, Australia.

TUESDAY 7TH MAY 1946

Following a successful interview with the board, George Stevenson was offered, and accepted, the role of team manager. Sailor Hunter had decided to stand down from that position but would continue as club secretary. Hunter himself had signed Stevenson and recommended him to the board as his successor in control of playing matters. Stevenson had won the league title with the club in 1932 and would guide the team to victories in both domestic cups during his nine-year spell in charge.

TUESDAY 7TH MAY 2002

Italian Serie A side Chievo Verona played a fundraising match at Fir Park following the administration announcement. Fans of various clubs attended and watched the game, which was played in a very competitive spirit for an end of season friendly. Honours were even at the end as a late equaliser by James McFadden secured a 1-1 draw.

MONDAY 7TH MAY 2007

Maurice Malpas' reign at Motherwell threatened to descend into farce when the side were beaten 4-1 by Dunfermline Athletic. The result meant Motherwell were still not safe with two matches to go despite being a massive 16 points clear with a game in hand just five weeks earlier. Matters were made worse when Mark Reynolds and Scott McDonald were sent off and ruled out of the upcoming crunch game with St Mirren through suspension.

SATURDAY 8TH MAY 1993

Motherwell faced Falkirk in a relegation showdown at Fir Park knowing a win would guarantee Premier League football for another season. The Bairns needed a win to stay alive and were backed by a huge travelling support which almost filled the cavernous South Stand. Chris McCart gave Motherwell a first-half lead but Brian Rice's long shot set up a dramatic finale. Thankfully, it was Motherwell who delivered when Dougie Arnott made space for himself in the box and shot home via the far post to ensure survival.

SATURDAY 9TH MAY 1987

Motherwell formed a guard of honour as Dundee United took to the pitch at Fir Park in recognition of their participation in the Uefa Cup Final. The compliment ended there and winger Gordon Mair scored the only goal in a 1-0 win.

SATURDAY 9TH MAY 1998

Aberdeen won 2-1 at Fir Park in a game that saw several established players say farewell. Manager Harri Kampman decided a clearout was needed meaning fan favourites such as Brian Martin, Tommy Coyne and Dougie Arnott were shown the door. All three played in this match and John Philliben was also released at the end of the season.

SATURDAY 10TH MAY 1997

Going into this game with Dunfermline, Motherwell knew all that was needed to avoid a play-off with Airdrie was to match the result Hibs achieved against Raith Rovers. Hibs pulled back an early deficit and though they couldn't find a winner the draw looked to be enough for them as Motherwell were losing 2-1. However, when a hero was needed the captain stepped up and Mitchell van der Gaag sent a 30-yard free-kick screaming into the top corner to spark a pitch invasion and wild celebrations at the full-time whistle.

SATURDAY 10TH MAY 2003

An Ian Murray penalty at Easter Road gave Hibs a narrow victory over Motherwell and left the team staring relegation in the face. Stevie Craig missed a glorious late chance to snatch an equaliser but the real damage came elsewhere when Dundee United grabbed a last-minute winner at Livingston. That meant with only two games still to play Motherwell were four points behind the Tannadice side.

SATURDAY 10TH MAY 2008

European participation was all but secured when Aberdeen were beaten 2-1 at Fir Park thanks to goals from Darren Smith and Chris Porter. Third place was made official the following day when Hibs lost 2-0 at Celtic Park.

WEDNESDAY 11TH MAY 1927

Motherwell travelled to Spain for an end of season tour. In exchange for a guarantee of £1,700, a party of 16 players set off along with manager, trainer and guide to compete for the King of Spain and Barcelona Cups together with Barcelona, Real Madrid and Swansea while further games were organised against a Bilbao select and Celta Vigo.

TUESDAY 11TH MAY 1965

The prolific Joe McBride handed in a transfer request which was turned down by the board. However, he would not have to wait too long for his move and soon went to Celtic as Jock Stein's first signing as manager for £22,000.

SATURDAY 11TH MAY 1985

Motherwell were already promoted but returned to the Premier League in style by winning the First Division. The title was secured on the last day of the season thanks to a 0-0 draw at Station Park, Forfar.

SATURDAY 12TH MAY 1945

A year after winning at Hampden in the Summer Cup, Motherwell returned to face Rangers in the Southern League Cup Final. The Steelmen went down 2-1.

SATURDAY 12TH MAY 1984

Bobby Watson's last match in charge was the final game of the 1983/84 season. The team had performed dismally in the league and with only one win arriving in the last ten games it was no surprise relegation was the result. Watson resigned soon after yet another defeat.

SATURDAY 12TH MAY 2007

Motherwell entertained St Mirren in a six-point clash at the bottom of the SPL. Despite leading 2-0 shortly after half-time, Motherwell were badly outfought as the Buddies stormed back to win 3-2. Only Dunfermline losing in Inverness prevented a nerve-shredding last day in Dundee and ensured the team's safety. The fans protested loudly against Maurice Malpas at full-time, displaying banners and throwing season tickets onto the pitch.

SUNDAY 13TH MAY 1962

As part of the earlier arrangement to play Nimes at Fir Park, a trip to France was scheduled for the end of the season. Motherwell drew with the French champions but they also travelled south to take on Marseille. L'OM were not the force they would become in the 1990s and were soundly beaten 4-1 by the touring party.

SATURDAY 13TH MAY 2000

The European battle continued when Motherwell faced Dundee United at Tannadice and Hearts travelled to Ibrox. Rangers picked up the three points meaning Motherwell could set up a last day of drama with a win on Tayside. Don Goodman's first-half goal was equalised but The Don was not to be denied and prodded home a late winner.

MONDAY 14TH MAY 1923

Permission was given to manager John Hunter to sign George Stevenson from Kilbirnie Ladeside. Stevenson agreed to join and started a 32-year love affair with the club which saw him pick up the league title as a player and both domestic cups as manager.

FRIDAY 14TH MAY 1971

An old timer charity game took place at Fir Park between former professionals representing East and West. Several Motherwell heroes featured including Andy Paton, Archie Shaw, Willie Redpath and Hastie Weir as the sides battled to a spirited 3-3 draw.

SATURDAY 14TH MAY 1994

Spectators were allowed to stand for the last time at Fir Park for the 1-0 home defeat by St Johnstone. The result allowed Aberdeen to take second place, leaving Motherwell in third, still the best performance for over thirty years. There was a feeling of what might have been though as Rangers won the title with only four points more than Motherwell's total of 54. This also turned out to be Tommy McLean's last game in charge as he failed to agree a new contract over the summer and moved to Hearts.

SATURDAY 15TH MAY 1982

Motherwell were already promoted when they travelled to Tynecastle for the last game of the 1981/82 season. Hearts were looking to grab the second promotion spot but needed a win to stand a chance. Unfortunately for them, Motherwell won 1-0, leading to ugly clashes with the home support both during the game and at full-time.

SATURDAY 15TH MAY 1993

Motherwell visited Broomfield for the last time in 1993. As Airdrie were one of the sides relegated while 'Well survived, the visiting fans were in party mood and a 2-1 win did nothing to dampen their spirits. Broomfield was later sold to a supermarket chain and Airdrie eventually moved to a new purpose-built ground.

MONDAY 15TH MAY 1995

Colin O'Neil enjoyed a testimonial match against Ipswich Town which ended in a 3-2 victory for Motherwell. O'Neil played the first few minutes and even set up the first goal with an exquisite chip. 'Psycho', as he was affectionately known, patrolled the Motherwell midfield 64 times on league business but will be best remembered for his winning penalty in the cup run at Morton, and his long-range goal in the semi-final.

WEDNESDAY 16TH MAY 1990

Davie Cooper picked up the last of his 22 Scotland caps in the 3-1 home defeat to Egypt. Cooper looked set to be the first Motherwell player to go to the World Cup after an outstanding season brought him back into Andy Roxburgh's plans, but injury meant he was denied a place in the squad for Italy.

WEDNESDAY 16TH MAY 2001

Gary McAllister, who came through the Motherwell youth system, was part of the Liverpool side which completed the cup treble. McAllister scored a penalty in the Uefa Cup Final and set up the winning golden goal against Alaves while he also played in the League Cup and FA Cup Final wins over Birmingham City and Arsenal.

MONDAY 17TH MAY 1886

Motherwell came into existence on this day in 1886 as members of local clubs Alpha and Glencairn met in Baillie's Pub in Merry Street. It was decided to form a completely new club named Motherwell FC and a combined team, though heavily dominated by Alpha players, was soon fielded against Hamilton.

SATURDAY 17TH MAY 2003

There was tension in the air at Fir Park when Motherwell took on Aberdeen. The side was in desperate relegation trouble and needed a win to keep any chance of survival alive. However, the result – a 3-2 defeat – was made irrelevant as Dundee United won at Partick Thistle, thus condemning 'Well to bottom spot. Nevertheless, relegation could still be avoided if Falkirk failed in their bid to have the SPL rules changed to allow them promotion without a compliant stadium.

SUNDAY 18TH MAY 1975

Colin McAdam became Motherwell's record signing when he arrived from Dumbarton for a reported fee of nearly £50,000. The versatile player could operate both in defence and attack but could notch only three league goals during his spell at Fir Park. He moved to Partick Thistle and scored freely, suggesting that Motherwell might have received a better return by using him differently.

SATURDAY 18TH MAY 1991

After a wait of 39 years, a major trophy finally returned to Lanarkshire when Motherwell lifted the Scottish Cup. The final against Dundee United capped an amazing run and this game was one of the best ever witnessed at Hampden. Despite United having a goal disallowed and hitting the post, Iain Ferguson put Motherwell in front at the break. Ally Maxwell was badly injured, suffering a ruptured spleen, but played on heroically as goals from Phil O'Donnell and Ian Angus put one hand on the trophy. Darren Jackson equalised in injury time so it was left to super sub Steve Kirk to head the winner in extra time.

SATURDAY 19TH MAY 1894

Scottish football history is littered with clubs which fell by the wayside. On this day in 1894 the ambiguously named Northern were beaten 2-0 by Motherwell at Dalziel Park.

THURSDAY 19TH MAY 1927

The highlight of the Spanish tour was possibly the second match, when Motherwell took on Real Madrid. The hosts were soundly beaten 3-1 with goals coming from Davie Hutcheson, Bobby Ferrier and Craig Thackery giving Motherwell a famous victory. The side were awarded the King of Spain Cup after the game for their efforts.

WEDNESDAY 19TH MAY 1971

Motherwell captain Bobby Watson was named Player of the Year at an event in the Fir Park Club. Watson later served as manager but is more fondly remembered as a player.

SUNDAY 19TH MAY 1991

Thousands of people lined the streets of Motherwell to salute the conquering cup heroes. An open-top bus carried the players, wives and staff – along with the trophy – around the town. Davie Cooper, who had won numerous honours but never taken part in a similar celebration, later said it was one of the high points of his career.

SATURDAY 19TH MAY 2007

It was not known at the time but a dull 0-0 draw at Dundee United would be the last game of the Maurice Malpas era. Under his stewardship the side finished tenth in the table and only escaped relegation on the second last day of the season after a diabolical run delivered a mere seven points from the last 36 available.

MONDAY 20TH MAY 2002

James McFadden earned his first Scotland cap against South Africa in an end of season tour of Hong Kong. Unfortunately, the first big headlines James made as a national player came when he missed the flight home following a night out! Despite that early setback, his Scotland career has blossomed with several goals being scored, including a sensational winner in Paris.

SATURDAY 21st MAY 1904

The first manager and club secretary to be appointed was P B Macdonald, who was chosen from 288 applicants. The ex-Newcastle and Sunderland amateur was not suited to the job and left in October of the same year.

FRIDAY 21st MAY 1965

The *Motherwell Times* complimented groundsman Archie Shaw on his excellent work in keeping the park in trim. A hectic schedule of games posed problems, on one occasion forcing Archie and his helpers to work under the floodlights until around midnight.

SUNDAY 21st MAY 1995

Three Motherwell players represented Scotland together in the Kirin Cup tie with Japan. Rob McKinnon, Brian Martin and Paul Lambert all featured in the side which drew 0-0.

SUNDAY 21st MAY 2000

The European challenge came to a bittersweet end when Rangers were defeated 2-0 but the side narrowly missed out on third spot. Hearts defeated Hibs to claim the Uefa Cup place.

SATURDAY 22nd MAY 1886

Motherwell's first game was a victory over Hamilton. Jock McPherson, Alex Kemp and James Murray goals secured a 3-2 win at Roman Road.

SUNDAY 22nd MAY 1927

The tour of Spain continued with a 2-2 draw against Barcelona. Coupled with two defeats of Swansea City, this was enough to secure more silverware in the shape of the Barcelona Cup.

SUNDAY 22nd MAY 2005

Celtic came to Fir Park needing a last day win to collect the championship. They led at half-time but there was drama to come. Scott McDonald hooked home a late equaliser and as Celtic pushed forward he struck another on the break. That was enough to break Celtic hearts as the title went to Rangers.

PAUL LAMBERT ON SCOTLAND DUTY

FRIDAY 23rd MAY 1975

Bobby Graham hit back at the club through the media for claiming his wage demands were extortionate. Willie Pettigrew had recently agreed new terms but Graham was unable to come to an agreement and was transfer listed. A deal was eventually reached and Graham continued at Fir Park until the summer of 1977.

SUNDAY 23rd MAY 1999

Motherwell fans were in boisterous mood on the last day of the season at East End Park. Late goals by Don Goodman and Dougie Ramsey gave the team victory over already-relegated Dunfermline before chairman John Boyle marched across the pitch to greet the away fans. Hopes were high for the next season as Boyle attempted to turn Motherwell into Scottish football's third force.

FRIDAY 23rd MAY 2003

The SPL decided that stadium requirements could not be waived to allow Falkirk promotion, meaning Motherwell would retain their place in the SPL for the 2003/04 season. However, the elation was short-lived as Falkirk quickly announced they would appeal against the decision.

MONDAY 24th MAY 1887

The first Motherwell annual meeting was held in 1887. Fees were set at 6/- for playing members while honorary members were able to watch every game for 3/-.

WEDNESDAY 24th MAY 1967

Charlie Aitken enjoyed a testimonial against Rangers in recognition of his 17 years of service. The match ended 1-1 as the powerful wing-half waved farewell to Fir Park. He made 313 league appearances during his time at the club but missed out on both cup wins in the 1950s, collecting only one winner's medal in the 1965 Summer Cup.

SATURDAY 24th MAY 2003

After the SPL decision to deny Falkirk promotion, Motherwell celebrated in joyous fashion by thrashing Livingston. A majestic second half hat-trick from James McFadden, which included a penalty and a glorious 60 yard run and finish, led the team to a 6-2 win.

SATURDAY 25TH MAY 1957

Future Motherwell manager Mark McGhee was born in Glasgow on this day in 1957. His playing career started with Morton and took in spells at Newcastle (twice), Aberdeen, Hamburg, Celtic, Brage and Reading before he went into management at the end of his playing career at Elm Park. He had picked up several domestic honours and also set up the winning goal for John Hewitt when Aberdeen won the 1983 Cup Winners' Cup in Gothenburg.

MONDAY 26TH MAY 2008

Mark McGhee's wonderful first season in charge of Motherwell quickly had other suitors calling. Scotland interviewed him and then it looked certain Hearts would take him to Tynecastle. However, as he was about to board a plane to finalise details of the job with Vladimir Romanov, he decided instead his future lay at Fir Park. Motherwell fans were delighted when he announced he would stay having agreed an improved deal.

WEDNESDAY 26TH MAY 1965

Motherwell reached the final of the Summer Cup with a sensational second leg semi-final performance against Hibs. Trailing 2-0 from the first game at Easter Road, goals from Andy Weir and Joe McBride helped the side produce a 3-1 win in normal time. Extra time was needed to separate the teams and it was Motherwell who came out on top, with Pat Delaney (2) and Charlie Aitken the goalscoring heroes.

SATURDAY 27TH MAY 1995

Two ex-Motherwell stars earned Scottish Cup winners medals at Hampden Park. Tom Boyd and Phil O'Donnell both played for Celtic in the 1-0 win over Airdrie while future 'Well players Gordon Marshall, Willie Falconer and Paul Harvey also featured.

WEDNESDAY 28TH MAY 1997

Former Motherwell midfielder Paul Lambert picked up a Champions League winner's medal with Borussia Dortmund. Lambert turned into an excellent holding midfielder and played alongside world-class players such as Mathias Sammer and Andreas Möller as Dortmund defeated Juventus 3-1 in Munich.

SATURDAY 29TH MAY 1965

Shortly after being taken to extra time by Hibs in the Fir Park semi-final, Dundee United visited Motherwell for the first leg of the Summer Cup final. United were dispatched confidently as the Steelmen took a 3-1 advantage to Tayside for the return match, with Pat Delaney (2) and Joe McBride getting on the scoresheet while only Finn Dossing could reply for the Terrors.

SUNDAY 29TH MAY 1977

Motherwell produced a sensational performance to beat Ajax 4-2 in an end of season friendly. The illustrious side won the Eredivisie that year and contained both Wim Suurbier and Ruud Krol who would play in the World Cup Final in Argentina in 1978. The occasion was seen as a let down, though, as Motherwell paid Ajax £12,000 but only enticed 7,535 through the turnstiles.

MONDAY 30TH MAY 1904

P B Macdonald enjoyed his first day in the job as Motherwell manager. However, perhaps it is not surprising he was not overly successful – although he had some experience in the game, his previous job was with a telephone company in Liverpool.

SATURDAY 30TH MAY 1953

Fir Park staged its first schoolboy international in 15 years when Scotland faced Wales. Billy Reid got Scotland's goal in a 1-1 draw and would later sign for Motherwell, his home-town team.

FRIDAY 30TH MAY 2008

A drought of 32 years was ended when a Motherwell player finally scored for Scotland. Willie Pettigrew was the last to have that honour but David Clarkson found the net against the Czech Republic in Prague. Clarkson came on as a substitute but despite his goal, the hosts won 3-1.

FRIDAY 31ST MAY 1895

The last game at Dalziel Park was when Royal Albert visited on a Friday evening. The aim of the challenge game was to raise funds for the new park and takings from the gate contributed £12 towards the project.

MOTHERWELL FC
On This Day

JUNE

TUESDAY 1st JUNE 2004

Keith Lasley had proved himself to be a solid midfielder after coming through the Fir Park youth system and he was tempted down to Plymouth Argyle on a free transfer when his contract expired. However, Lasley didn't really settle on the south coast and later returned to Motherwell, where he had remained popular with the fans.

FRIDAY 1st JUNE 2007

Maurice Malpas left his post as manager, leaving the club searching for a new boss. The team under Malpas had a terrible end to the previous season but he was determined to hold his ground. This changed when owner John Boyle announced assistant manager Paul Hegarty would be sacked to make way for Scott Leitch and Malpas resigned in protest.

WEDNESDAY 2nd JUNE 1965

Motherwell won their first competition of note for 12 years when the Summer Cup was collected at Tannadice. Leading 3-1 from the first leg, Motherwell managed to hold on to lose only 1-0 to Dundee United, ensuring an aggregate win. Captain Pat Delaney was carried shoulder high by his teammates after receiving the trophy and a crowd quickly gathered at Motherwell Cross to await the arrival of the team. However, the players stayed overnight in Dundee but the local population was able to indulge in celebrations the following day.

SATURDAY 3rd JUNE 1995

A double from Roy Essandoh gave the youth team a 2-0 win over Monthey in a tournament in Switzerland. This allowed the side to top their qualifying group and proceed to the final the next day, which they lost to Real Madrid.

SUNDAY 4th JUNE 1922

A representative from Manchester City attended a Fir Park board meeting with a view to purchasing Hugh Ferguson. After offers were batted to and fro, a fee of £3,900 was agreed, only for the striker to make it all a waste of time by declining the move anyway!

TUESDAY 5th JUNE 1923

An EGM was called by secretary John Hunter to issue an additional 1,000 shares in the club. They were initially offered to existing shareholders before new investors had the chance to purchase any that were left over as the club attempted to raise more money.

MONDAY 5th JUNE 1939

Ben Ellis was appointed captain for the forthcoming season. However, the honour was made somewhat redundant by the outbreak of the Second World War which caused the cancellation of the league after only a handful of fixtures had been completed.

THURSDAY 5th JUNE 2003

Terry Butcher strengthened the team for the following campaign by snapping up three players on free transfers. Former 'Well stars Alex Burns and Stephen Craigan re-signed from Partick Thistle while veteran goalkeeper Gordon Marshall joined from Kilmarnock. The Firhill side were particularly bitter at the loss of two of their better players to a club still operating in administration.

WEDNESDAY 6th JUNE 1945

A board meeting granted permission for the manager to sign 17-year-old forward Wilson Humphries. He would become a vital part of the team for several years to come but could have made even more than his 199 league appearances had it not been for his national service.

TUESDAY 7th JUNE 1928

A year after the successful tour of Spain, Motherwell went further afield with a visit to Argentina, Uruguay and Brazil. After the long journey the team were slow to recover and lost the first three games but won the next six, including this 3-2 victory over Argentinians Rosario thanks to goals by Willie McFadyen, George Stevenson and Alex McMurtie.

FRIDAY 8th JUNE 2007

Brian Kerr took to the media to criticise the club. The midfielder, who had recently moved to Hibs on a free transfer, said Maurice Malpas was put in an impossible position by budget constraints, and the fact that Motherwell would always be a selling club.

SATURDAY 9TH JUNE 1934

The touring bug had well and truly infected Motherwell and a mammoth 16-game trip to South Africa and Rhodesia was undertaken in the summer of 1934. Every game was won with Willie McFadyen being the main scoring hero. In a contest with Mashonaland on this day he grabbed five goals in a 6-0 win while Duncan Ogilvie notched the other strike.

SATURDAY 10TH JUNE 1933

It was decided by the board to accept an offer to play two exhibition matches in Paris the following year. The club had been guaranteed £600 for agreeing to the deal.

SUNDAY 10TH JUNE 1951

Even the losers in cup finals are rewarded and the board received a cheque for the club's share of the gate from the Hampden Park defeat to Celtic. The finances were boosted by more than £6,000.

SATURDAY 10TH JUNE 1965

After making it clear for some time that he wanted a transfer, Joe McBride finally got what he wanted when he was signed by Celtic for £22,000. The prolific scorer had recently contributed to the Summer Cup win by scoring against every side Motherwell faced.

FRIDAY 10TH JUNE 1994

An era ended at Fir Park when Tommy McLean resigned his position as manager. After finishing third in the league the previous season – the best performance since 1959 – it was a bitter blow to lose McLean who had been in charge since 1984. He had immediately guided the side back into the Premier League and to Scottish Cup glory in 1991 but left after disagreements with the board over the future direction of the club.

SUNDAY 11TH JUNE 1995

Tommy Coyne equalled a 60-year long record when he collected 12 international caps as a Motherwell player. His appearance for Ireland in the 3-1 home defeat to Austria matched George Stevenson's tally of 12 Scotland games, the last of which came in 1935.

THURSDAY 12TH JUNE 1975

The board arranged a special meeting to discuss a proposed tour of Ecuador and Colombia. Motherwell would be expected to play five games in the July trip but careful consideration had to be given to the disruption it would cause the pre-season preparations and this eventually caused the offer to be turned down.

SATURDAY 13TH JUNE 1931

The highlight of the South African tour came when 29,000 watched Motherwell take on South Africa in Johannesburg. The tourists were simply a class above their hosts on this day and crushed them 8-0 with Willie McFadyen scoring six of the goals. Earlier and later tests also ended in victory for the Steelmen.

FRIDAY 13TH JUNE 1975

An excited *Motherwell Times*, unaware of the decision to turn down the tour of South America, made reference to the previous tours carried out in the 1920s and 30s. They may have taken things a little too far by suggesting: '…the South Americans always maintain that their knowledge of advanced football came from Motherwell FC.'

TUESDAY 14TH JUNE 1927

The Motherwell touring party returned from Spain by boat with slightly more luggage than when they departed. The King of Spain and Barcelona Cups had been picked up on the successful journey which included a win over Real Madrid and a draw with Catalan giants Barcelona.

MONDAY 14TH JUNE 1999

It was announced John Swinburne was to be given a place on the board. The soon-to-be retired commercial manager had been involved at Fir Park for years and had written various books about the club.

SATURDAY 15TH JUNE 1996

Scotland lost 2-0 to England at Euro 96. There were several Motherwell connections in the Scottish team that day, most notably Gary McAllister, who didn't have a game to remember, though, as he missed a penalty with the game still in the balance.

FRIDAY 16TH JUNE 1911

On this day Bobby Ancell was born in Dumfries. He had a solid playing career which was effectively brought to an end by the Second World War. He then moved into management and brought fame and admiration, if not trophies, to Motherwell in his time at Fir Park.

TUESDAY 16TH JUNE 1959

Before the 55th AGM, most of the shareholders watched a training session. Sailor Hunter was present and received glowing tributes for his 48-year association with the club. The club had also taken on a lease of the Motherwell Stadium to extend training facilities and a start had been made that week to lay concrete steps on the terracing.

THURSDAY 17TH JUNE 1954

The 50th AGM resolved to improve the facilities for supporters. Plans to build a covered enclosure along with a new tea bar were discussed.

FRIDAY 17TH JUNE 1955

The Scottish Football League met to decide on reconstruction. The motion for the top league to be expanded to 18 teams from 16 was carried by 25 votes to 12 which meant rather than being relegated, Motherwell would stay in 'A' Division for the season to come.

SATURDAY 18TH JUNE 1994

Tommy Coyne became the first Motherwell man to play at the World Cup finals. He played in the Republic of Ireland's dramatic 1-0 win over Italy which helped them qualify for the knockout phase.

TUESDAY 18TH JUNE 2002

Despite being in administration, Motherwell managed to secure a vital source of revenue in the form of a new shirt sponsor. Local decorating firm The Untouchables moved in to replace Motorola.

MONDAY 18TH JUNE 2007

Following the dismissal of Maurice Malpas, Mark McGhee was appointed as the new manager. McGhee had been a very successful striker with Aberdeen and Celtic in Scotland but his previous management experience had all come south of the border.

THE GREAT JOHN 'SAILOR' HUNTER.

MONDAY 19th JUNE 1953

A strange motion was defeated at the 53rd AGM at Fir Park. It was suggested the shareholders turn over their 20 per cent dividend to the manager to spend on players but the majority preferred to receive their cut of the club's profits.

THURSDAY 19th JUNE 2003

The SPL decided Falkirk's appeal to be admitted to the league could be heard. They had initially been refused promotion as their stadium was not compliant. This meant the Scottish Football League published their own fixtures with 'Club X' as they waited to see if Falkirk or Motherwell would take the place. Motherwell were also entered into the Challenge Cup for the only time in their history: the draw gave Falkirk/Motherwell a long trip north to Brechin City in the first round.

WEDNESDAY 20th JUNE 1984

New manager Tommy McLean wasted no time in strengthening the squad for the First Division. Derek Murray was his first signing with the left-back costing £5,000 from Dundee United.

FRIDAY 21st JUNE 1935

The Malvera Bowling Club in Johannesburg was so impressed by Motherwell on a recent tour of South Africa that they adopted claret and amber as their official colours. However, they could not find a suitable flag so requested that secretary Sailor Hunter send off a version similar to that which flew over Fir Park.

TUESDAY 21st JUNE 1994

A public meeting was held in the Carousel Bar, Bellshill, to discuss the situation at Motherwell following Tommy McLean's departure. The assembly was originally intended to create a new supporters' club from the bar but was opened up to everyone in view of recent events.

MONDAY 22nd JUNE 1987

After a long pursuit, Jamie Fairlie was finally signed from Clydebank for £26,000. Fairlie is better known for successful spells at Hamilton but he did contribute a wonderful winner in a League Cup quarter-final victory over Hibs.

TUESDAY 23rd JUNE 1931

Motherwell's summer tour of South Africa brought an astonishing 14 wins from 15 games. One of the most convincing victories was against Eastern Province when Willie McFadyen (2), Bobby Ferrier (2), George Stevenson and John McMenemy scored in a 6-1 win.

FRIDAY 23rd JUNE 1967

The *Wishaw Press* reported that Motherwell feared losing John Martis for nothing. The defender was considering an offer from Chicago Spurs, but since they were a rebel club outside the official structure, they would not have to pay a fee for his services.

SUNDAY 24th JUNE 1928

Motherwell completed their South American tour with a 5-0 loss to Brazil in front of 40,000 in Rio. The return journey was a little tighter than planned as the players raced to the harbour still in their kit to ensure they got aboard the boat home!

FRIDAY 25th JUNE 1965

The *Motherwell Times* poked fun at the transfer saga involving Willie Hunter. A cartoon showed a customer in a record store asking if 'Set Me Free' from The Kinks, was actually by the Motherwell star!

SATURDAY 25th JUNE 2005

Graeme Smith signed on a free transfer from Rangers as back up to veteran Gordon Marshall. However, an injury to Marshall early in the season gave Smith the ideal opportunity to take over in goals.

THURSDAY 26th JUNE 2003

The SPL finally rejected Falkirk's request to be promoted without a compliant ground. The meeting had originally started the previous day but with no conclusion in sight it was agreed to adjourn until the next evening. Shortly before midnight, Motherwell were confirmed in the SPL despite finishing in the relegation spot. With the club in administration, the financial impact of this decision cannot be underestimated. It could be argued that the following period of relative success achieved by the club – a cup final and European football – started on this crucial day.

FRIDAY 27th JUNE 1997

A transfer saga of immense proportions began when Motherwell announced the signings of Franz Resch and Mario Dorner from VfB Modling. Motherwell believed the players to be available on a free transfer but this was later contested by the Austrian club.

SATURDAY 27th JUNE 1998

A prodigal son returned to Fir Park when veteran Brian McClair signed on a free transfer. McClair was successful with Celtic and Manchester United after leaving Motherwell but struggled to adapt to the pace of the SPL. He was soon allowed to join Blackburn Rovers as coach.

THURSDAY 28th JUNE 1979

Ally McLeod decided he needed a full-time keeper spelling the end for Stuart Rennie at Fir Park. He was swapped as part of the deal for Ayr United custodian Hugh Sproat. The eccentric Sproat soon showed a fondness for swinging on the bar and venturing upfield.

FRIDAY 29th JUNE 1984

Being a football manager brings many honours off the field. The Eagle Inn pub in Motherwell had been refurbished and Tommy McLean was the guest of honour to pull the first pint in the new look bar.

THURSDAY 29th JUNE 2000

A tabloid newspaper suggested that a £500,000 deal to buy Airdrie's ground, the Excelsior Stadium, would soon be completed. Airdrie were in financial difficulty and their administrators, KPMG, made the offer to Motherwell as the centrepiece of a proposed new football academy.

TUESDAY 30th JUNE 1991

Following the departure of captain Tom Boyd, the cup-winning side would see further changes. Tommy McLean withdrew contract offers to Craig Paterson and Ally Maxwell when deals couldn't be reached.

TUESDAY 30th JUNE 1998

Harri Kampman continued to rebuild the side and paraded several new signings at Fir Park. Sadly, only Jamie McGowan made any impact as Kampman underestimated what was required for Scottish football.

MOTHERWELL FC
On This Day

JULY

THURSDAY 1st JULY 1920

After consulting with Rangers manager Bill Struth, the Motherwell board decide to appoint C J Mears as trainer. It was the first time this position had been filled at Fir Park.

MONDAY 1st JULY 1991

With Alistair Maxwell embroiled in a bitter contract dispute, manager Tommy McLean wanted to find a replacement goalkeeper. Dundee United veteran Billy Thomson was signed and had a reliable season before eventually moving to Rangers having lost out to Sieb Dykstra in the battle for the number one spot.

SATURDAY 2nd JULY 1955

Due to the side struggling to keep their place in the top division following promotion, it was decided manager George Stevenson should be asked to resign and he did so on this day. It brought to an end a 32-year relationship between Stevenson and the club, leaving the club secretary, John Hunter, as the only notable connection remaining to the championship-winning side of 1932.

MONDAY 3rd JULY 2000

Motherwell bought a ten per cent stake in the northern English non-league side Workington Reds. The idea behind the purchase was to extend the youth and scouting programme into the north of England but the move was not overly successful and the link between the clubs was quietly dropped.

TUESDAY 3rd JULY 2007

Oldham Athletic striker Chris Porter signed for Motherwell on a free transfer. As it was a cross border move, Motherwell were not required to pay a fee for the player as an English club would have done. Porter enjoyed a great first season, bagging 18 goals.

SATURDAY 4th JULY 1977

Season tickets for the coming year went on sale at Fir Park. Adult prices ranged from £18 for the ground to £30 for the stand. There was a special offer for a husband and wife stand ticket at just £55 although cynics may question if a partner would be wanted at the football!

SUNDAY 5TH JULY 1987

Legendary manager Bobby Ancell died aged 76. He became Motherwell's third manager when he took over from George Stevenson in 1955 and in ten years at Fir Park earned the side a reputation for playing positive and attacking football. Nicknamed the Ancell Babes, the team came up just short in both league and major cup competitions but Motherwell fans still have fond memories of this time.

MONDAY 5TH JULY 1999

Motherwell finally signed Falkirk defender Martyn Corrigan. The fee would later be decided by tribunal and was set at £30,000. Corrigan would become a crucial part of the team but failed to regain his form after injury and left to join Kilmarnock in January 2008.

MONDAY 6TH JULY 1987

Chairman Ian Livingstone and vice-chair Malcolm McNeil resigned after a boardroom dispute. Both men objected to Hamish Deans being appointed to the board but they were outvoted. Local butcher John Chapman took over as chairman.

THURSDAY 6TH JULY 1989

Tommy McLean hit out in the media at the Fraser Wishart transfer saga. Wishart was determined to leave Fir Park but when a move to Celtic fell through he had to settle for a switch to St Mirren. However, the Paisley club were in decline after a strong period in the 1980s.

THURSDAY 7TH JULY 1927

The shareholders were presented with the trophies won in Spain at the AGM but there were more serious matters to discuss. The economic downturn in the local area, combined with the early exit from the Scottish Cup and the creation of a reserve team caused a financial loss for the year.

SATURDAY 8TH JULY 1944

Motherwell added the Summer Cup to the trophy cabinet when they defeated Clyde 1-0 at Hampden. The Summer Cup was not the most important of competitions but the wartime success helped overcome the ghosts of three Scottish Cup final losses at Hampden.

FRIDAY 9TH JULY 1993

Miodrag Krivokapic signed on a free transfer from Dundee United. Having been frozen out of the team by manager Jim McLean, younger brother Tommy snapped up the veteran defender. Mio was always calm on the ball and rarely resorted to thrashing clearances out of the ground, making him popular with the Fir Park support.

FRIDAY 10TH JULY 1998

Motherwell headed off to manager Harri Kampman's homeland for a pre-season tour. Despite winning the first game, two losses followed and this 2-0 reverse against FC Lahti caused consternation amongst the fans at home.

MONDAY 11TH JULY 1989

After financial struggles earlier in the decade, Motherwell were well on the way to recovery. The AGM was told of a trading profit for the fourth year in a row, with the club being £54,314 to the good.

THURSDAY 11TH JULY 1991

Motherwell's win in the Scottish Cup Final earned them a place in European competition for the first time. In the Geneva draw they were paired with GKS Katowice of Poland in the Cup Winners' Cup. They were the weakest seeded team available, but it meant Motherwell fans would have a gruelling journey if they wanted to follow the side to the away leg.

TUESDAY 11TH JULY 1995

Alex McLeish splashed the cash, spending £200,000 on John Hendry. Hendry had an impressive scoring record for Tottenham Hotspur reserves but was an unmitigated disaster at Fir Park, finding the net only three times in over 40 appearances before eventually being freed.

THURSDAY 11TH JULY 2002

Hull City took advantage of Motherwell being in administration to buy Stuart Elliot for £230,000. The Northern Irishman could play up front or out wide and scored frequently, especially in a side which was struggling more often than not. He did well at Hull initially but lost his place as they worked their way up the English leagues.

WEDNESDAY 12TH JULY 1995

Motherwell were paired with MyPa 47 in the qualifying round of the Uefa Cup. The Finns had a number of players who would go on to play with big clubs in Europe and, crucially, were already well into their domestic season giving them an edge in match sharpness.

WEDNESDAY 13TH JULY 1949

Motherwell won the five-a-side tournament held as part of the YMCA sports event at Fir Park. Several races and a javelin contest formed the athletics section while eight teams took part in the football. Motherwell defeated Hamilton 2-0 in the final with Andy Paton and Jimmy Watson getting the goals.

WEDNESDAY 13TH JULY 1994

The Motherwell board stunned Scottish football by appointing Aberdeen player Alex McLeish as Tommy McLean's replacement. McLeish guided the team to the runners-up spot in his first season but then struggled to maintain previous high standards. Remarkably, Guus Hiddink applied for the job but wasn't even granted an interview despite winning the European Cup with PSV: the lack of Scottish football knowledge made him unsuitable!

FRIDAY 14TH JULY 1978

Pre-season training resumed at Fir Park and contained someone who would become a well-known face in the background of Scottish football. Alan Mackin was a new signing for Motherwell but didn't make an impact at the club. However, he went on to become a director at East Stirlingshire.

FRIDAY 14TH JULY 1995

The new Davie Cooper Stand suffered storm damage. Around £5,000 worth of damage was done to carpets, curtains and tiles.

MONDAY 15TH JULY 1968

Cup-winning legend Wilson Humphries returned to Fir Park in a coaching capacity. He was on hand to help as pre-season training started but throughout the year he would work on a part-time basis, combining the role with his job as an English teacher at Dalziel High.

TUESDAY 16TH JULY 1968

Despite dropping into the Second Division, Motherwell were hopeful of maintaining crowds with the prospect of more wins! Stand season tickets went on sale at only £5.

TUESDAY 17TH JULY 2001

Fresh from a training camp in France, Motherwell ventured across the county to take on Albion Rovers at Cliftonhill. Goals from Kevin Twaddle and Stuart Elliot gave the visitors a 2-0 win but there would be disappointment to come when the season started for real.

TUESDAY 18TH JULY 1989

Striker Nick Cusack signed from Peterborough United but despite a good scoring record, disciplinary problems blighted his time at Fir Park. He was eventually sold to Darlington.

TUESDAY 19TH JULY 1932

Charlie Aitken was born in Gorebridge in 1932. He joined Motherwell in 1949 but the wing-half hadn't made his debut when the League Cup was won in 1950 and missed the 1952 Scottish Cup final completing his national service. Despite these disappointments, Aitken played 313 league games for the club and won the Summer Cup in 1965.

FRIDAY 19TH JULY 1974

Motherwell prepared to leave on a pre-season tour of West Germany and Denmark amid speculation over the boss's future. Ian St John had been contacted by Leeds about the vacancy at Elland Road, but he assured Motherwell his attention remained on the job at Fir Park.

SATURDAY 19TH JULY 2003

Motherwell visited New Douglas Park for the first time in a 2003 friendly. Hamilton impressed against their neighbours and it took a goal from Derek Adams to spare Motherwell's blushes in a 1-1 draw.

MONDAY 19TH JULY 1993

Dutch defender Luc Nijholt left to join Swindon Town in a deal worth £250,000. Nijholt had been signed by Tommy McLean for around £100,000 in 1990 and made a big contribution to the club.

TUESDAY 20TH JULY 1993

Following the departure of Nijholt, Tommy McLean moved quickly to replace him with Rab Shannon. A fee of £85,000 secured his signature from Dunfermline Athletic and he did a good job at right-back as Motherwell finished third and second in his first seasons at the club.

SUNDAY 21ST JULY 1985

Future captain Paul Quinn was born in Wishaw. Quinn came through the ranks at Fir Park and was handed the captain's armband after the tragic death of Phil O'Donnell.

FRIDAY 22ND JULY 1994

After two superb seasons in claret and amber, Sieb Dykstra attracted attention from the English Premiership. The eccentric Dutchman moved to Queens Park Rangers but his style did not fit at Loftus Road. He later returned to Scotland with Dundee United but remains popular with the Motherwell fans and frequently returns for 'old timer' charity and testimonial games.

TUESDAY 22ND JULY 1997

Chris McCart was allowed to join Falkirk on a free transfer in recognition of his service to the club. He had come through the youth system and won the Scottish Cup in 1991. After hanging up his boots Chris eventually found himself back at Fir Park as head of youth development before he took on a similar role at Celtic in summer 2008.

SATURDAY 23RD JULY 2005

Pre-season friendly games are more about the performance than result according to many managers but that would not have been much consolation to Terry Butcher. Queen of the South thrashed Motherwell 4-0 at Palmerston Park and such a heavy loss to a lower league side caused concern with the season scheduled to start a week later.

MONDAY 24TH JULY 1978

The team returned to Denmark to make their preparations for the forthcoming season. Frederickshavn of the First Division put up stern resistance but Jimmy Lindsay got the only goal of the game by converting a rebound from Willie Pettigrew's shot.

TUESDAY 25TH JULY 2000

A minor addition to the trophy cabinet arrived when Motherwell won the Motorola Cup. The technology company sponsored both Motherwell and Livingston and were responsible for arranging this pre-season friendly at Fir Park. The visitors marched through the leagues and eventually reached the SPL but on this occasion Motherwell were way too strong for them and won 6-1.

TUESDAY 26TH JULY 1927

The pre-season build up started with the team looking to improve on the runners-up spot of the previous year. There were 25 full-time players in the squad including new additions up front and on the wing in the form of Tom Tennant and Tom Douglas.

FRIDAY 26TH JULY 1974

A visit to cult team St Pauli in the workers' district of Hamburg would now be viewed as an ideal holiday for many Motherwell fans. There was considerably less fanfare when the sides met at the Millerntor in 1974 when goals from Ian Kennedy and Jim McCabe gave the guests an easy win over the Second Division side.

WEDNESDAY 27TH JULY 1977

Three years after the friendly meeting between the teams, Willie Pettigrew turned down a bumper move to German club St Pauli. Motherwell would have collected £300,000 in instalments but Pettigrew couldn't agree personal terms.

SATURDAY 27TH JULY 1991

Motherwell ran out at Elgin in a pre-season friendly with a new shirt sponsor. Ian Skelly had graced the shirts for several years but Motorola took over following the cup win in 1991. The international firm sponsored the side due to their local presence in Lanarkshire.

SATURDAY 28TH JULY 2001

Billy Davies, forced to rebuild the side after budget cuts, made a disastrous start to season 2001/02. A lightweight midfield played reasonably well in the first half at East End Park but fell apart after the break when Dunfermline romped to a convincing 5-2 win.

END OF THE SKELLY ERA: NOT ONLY DID FERGUSON'S GOAL SEND MOTHERWELL TO CUP GLORY, BUT INTO EUROPEAN COMPETITION AS WELL

SATURDAY 29TH JULY 2000

Dundee visited Fir Park for the opening game of the season with Ivano Bonetti in charge for the first time. Motherwell knew absolutely nothing about his hastily assembled team of foreigners and they were vastly superior to a Motherwell side hit by injury and suspension. The guests won 2-0 although it could easily have been a lot more.

TUESDAY 30TH JULY 1991

As Scottish Cup holders, Motherwell went on a tour of Germany to face a number of lower league sides. The final game was a 3-2 victory over Kickers Offenbach with Phil O'Donnell getting a double.

SATURDAY 30TH JULY 2005

Just a few weeks after losing the title at Motherwell, Celtic returned to Fir Park for a season opener. They seemed to have exorcised some demons when they led 3-1 at half-time but after a fantastic comeback put Motherwell 4-3 in front, the hosts looked set for the win. Sadly the Steelmen couldn't hold on and a last gasp Craig Beattie equaliser secured a 4-4 draw for the visitors.

SUNDAY 30TH JULY 2006

Maurice Malpas' first game in charge ended in a 2-1 defeat to Rangers. Despite an acrobatic equaliser from Phil O'Donnell, Motherwell were totally outplayed and could have no complaints about losing to Dado Prso's header.

SATURDAY 31ST JULY 1993

Blackburn Rovers had assembled an expensive squad when they travelled to Fir Park for a pre-season friendly. Dougie Arnott headed home the only goal of the game as Motherwell recorded a morale-boosting victory.

SATURDAY 31ST JULY 1999

Despite a bug sweeping Fir Park, Motherwell managed to secure an opening day draw at Easter Road. Pat Nevin scored an equaliser but Dirk Lehman's second goal seemed to give the hosts a victory. However, Steven Nicholas cut inside his man in injury time and fired home from an angle with the aid of a slight deflection.

MOTHERWELL FC
On This Day

AUGUST

THURSDAY 1st AUGUST 1895

Anticipation swept Motherwell before the new Fir Park stadium was opened. Around 1,000 people turned up to watch a bounce match featuring Motherwell players, two days ahead of the first fixture against Celtic.

SATURDAY 1st AUGUST 1903

The Lanarkshire Police Sports Day, featuring a range of track and field events, was held at Fir Park. A prize fund of £17 was on offer in the 5-a-side competition which saw Motherwell lose to Celtic by the curious score of 2 goals and 1 point to 1 point.

SATURDAY 1st AUGUST 1998

Harri Kampman's new-look side produced an opening day win over St Johnstone. Miko Kaven, Michael Doesburg, Jamie McGowan, Jan Michels, Rob Matthei and Jered Stirling all made debuts with Stirling curling home the winning free-kick.

FRIDAY 2nd AUGUST 1968

The legendary Joe Wark made his first appearance in a Motherwell jersey against Tranmere in a pre-season friendly. Things didn't go to plan as an early injury to 'keeper Keith MacRae meant Joe spent 87 minutes of the match in goals! He did keep a clean sheet though as Motherwell won 2-0.

THURSDAY 2nd AUGUST 1990

Luc Nijholt arrived at Fir Park and turned out to be one of Tommy McLean's best signings. The tough-tackling defender quickly became a favourite with the fans and played in the Scottish Cup-winning side of 1991. He also contributed goals from the penalty spot before being sold to Swindon Town in 1993.

SATURDAY 2nd AUGUST 1997

A fine double from Tommy Coyne gave Motherwell an opening-day win at East End Park. Dunfermline had been the better side in the first half but an improved performance after the break took the points to Lanarkshire.

SATURDAY 3RD AUGUST 1895

The first game at Fir Park ended in a convincing 8-1 loss to Celtic. There were around 5,500 in the ground and 600 in the small stand. The friendly nature of the game was shown by the club presidents running the lines.

MONDAY 3RD AUGUST 1953

Motherwell arranged a charity match between the squad members at Fir Park. However, the manager may have had cause to re-think his plans for the season when the 'Probables' lost 5-3 to the 'Possibles'!

THURSDAY 3RD AUGUST 1978

Left-back Joe Wark was honoured for his ten years' service with a testimonial game against West Brom. The visitors were far too strong for Motherwell and won 8-1 as Cyrille Regis and Laurie Cunningham ran riot. Wark holds the record for post-war league appearances with 469, but despite his consistent form he was inexplicably denied a full Scotland cap.

SATURDAY 3RD AUGUST 2002

Motherwell started the season in administration and a young team took to the field at Livingston for the opening game. Motherwell did well but not quite well enough – two goals late in the game could not recover a 3-0 deficit.

FRIDAY 4TH AUGUST 1989

A pre-season friendly showed hope for the months ahead as Spanish giants Real Sociedad were humbled 4-0 at Fir Park. Tommy McLean had been building the side up from relegation strugglers and was closing in on success.

SATURDAY 4TH AUGUST 2007

The Mark McGhee era kicked off with a 1-0 opening day win at Love Street. Steven McGarry scored a wonderful winner against St Mirren by finishing a fine move which consisted of several one touch passes. The determination to play good football delighted the visiting fans.

SATURDAY 5TH AUGUST 1893

The decision to turn professional had been heartily debated at the recent AGM but the board felt it was the only way to progress. Motherwell's first professional game was played on this day against Hamilton with the side winning 4-1.

SATURDAY 5TH AUGUST 1961

Dougie Arnott was born on this day in Carluke. The little striker was playing junior football until he was 25 when Tommy McLean decided to take a chance on him. Arnott eventually discovered an eye for goal and the fans loved him for his tenacious fighting spirit and constant running. He had a remarkable record against the Old Firm and bagged several goals against the Glasgow pair.

THURSDAY 5TH AUGUST 1971

Motherwell's proposed tour of Italy hit a glitch when railway repairs caused the team to miss their connection to Gatwick at St Pancras station. Despite taking a fleet of taxis to the airport the players missed the plane but fortunately the tour organiser managed to find seats on the flight to Genoa the next day.

SATURDAY 6TH AUGUST 1977

The Anglo-Scottish Cup produced a memorable game against lowly Alloa Athletic. An inspired Vic Davidson scored five goals in a 7-0 win which made the second leg a mere formality.

WEDNESDAY 7TH AUGUST 1895

After Celtic opened Fir Park by winning, Motherwell did not have long to wait to record a victory of their own. A few days later Clyde were duly beaten in a friendly and that put the team in good spirits. The first competitive win was a 2-1 success over Port Glasgow the following Saturday.

SATURDAY 7TH AUGUST 1993

After narrowly escaping the drop the previous year, a 2-2 draw at home to Celtic – with goals from Dougie Arnott and Alex Burns – was the start of happier times in 1993/94. The team would make a serious title challenge for the first time in more than thirty years.

SATURDAY 8TH AUGUST 1931

The press speculated Motherwell might finally break the Old Firm championship monopoly. Things started well in season 1931/32 with a 5-1 win at Queen's Park.

TUESDAY 8TH AUGUST 1995

Motherwell took part in the Uefa Cup for the second season in a row but Finnish team MyPa 47 put an early end to the campaign. Shaun McSkimming opened the scoring in the first leg at Fir Park but poor defending allowed the visitors to go home with a 3-1 lead.

SATURDAY 8TH AUGUST 1998

Cup final hero Steve Kirk returned to his first club East Fife as manager and his side were drawn against Motherwell in the League Cup. Motherwell won 1-0 in extra time in this last visit to old Bayview.

SATURDAY 9TH AUGUST 1947

Motherwell beat Queen of the South 4-0 in the first game of the League Cup group section. The match was notable for Motherwell wearing numbers on the backs of their shirts for the first time.

TUESDAY 9TH AUGUST 1994

Motherwell returned to European competition with a Uefa Cup preliminary round tie against Havnar Bóltfelag of the Faroe Islands. Goals from Tommy Coyne, Paul McGrillen and Steve Kirk gave Motherwell a convincing 3-0 first-leg lead.

FRIDAY 9TH AUGUST 1996

After a successful trial period, Paul Lambert signed for Borussia Dortmund on a free transfer. Alex McLeish speculated Lambert would become a bit-part player but he became an integral part of the Dortmund Champions League-winning team.

SATURDAY 10TH AUGUST 1946

After Sailor Hunter stood down as manager, it meant a new boss would be in charge for the first time in 35 years. George Stevenson moved into the manager's chair but his first match ended in defeat as Rangers won 4-2 at Fir Park despite two goals from John Brown.

SATURDAY 11TH AUGUST 1962

The brand new Main Stand was christened with a spectacular game against Falkirk in the League Cup. Bobby Ancell's babes were at the height of their powers and a simply devastating performance saw them go in for their half-time tea 9-0 up! Goals from Bobby Russell (5) and Pat Quinn (4) did the damage but the Bairns did manage to restore some dignity in the second period as the game ended 9-1.

SATURDAY 11TH AUGUST 1984

Tommy McLean took charge for the first time with a convincing 2-0 win over Kilmarnock. Only 2,384 fans turned out to watch the victory and it took some time before McLean developed a style of football that had punters flocking back to Fir Park.

FRIDAY 11TH AUGUST 1989

A wonderful piece of business from Tommy McLean secured the signature of Davie Cooper for a mere £50,000. The winger no longer featured in the first eleven plans at Rangers and moved to Motherwell to extend his playing career. While many suspected Cooper was winding down, he turned in a series of brilliant performances which took him back into the Scotland squad and helped the team to win the Scottish Cup in 1991.

SATURDAY AUGUST 12TH 1893

Motherwell made their league debut with a 4-1 win over Clyde. Having been elected to the league they were the only Lanarkshire team at the national level and finished fourth in the ten-team Second Division.

THURSDAY 12TH AUGUST 1965

Motherwell's team in the Lanarkshire Police Sports at Clyde's Shawfield Park was; Bert Howieson, Bobby McCallum, Matt Thomson, Willie McCallum and Willie Hunter. Rangers and Hamilton Accies were beaten but the final was lost to Celtic by three goals to a corner.

SATURDAY 12TH AUGUST 1989

Nick Cusack endeared himself to the Motherwell crowd on his debut by grabbing a goal at Tannadice and leaping into the crowd of celebrating 'Well fans.

SATURDAY 13th AUGUST 1932

There was a fine moment at Fir Park when the wife of chairman Tom Ormiston unveiled the Scottish Championship flag before the match against Kilmarnock. Motherwell could only draw 3-3.

SATURDAY 13th AUGUST 1955

Bobby Ancell took charge for the first time for the League Cup tie against Forfar. Ancell developed a famous attacking side – early evidence of that came as the Loons were dismantled 6-1.

SATURDAY 13th AUGUST 1966

Substitutes were allowed for the first time at the start of this season. Angus Moffat made history by being the first ever Motherwell player to enter a match from the bench and promptly grabbed another record too. Sadly, the first ever Motherwell goal by a substitute counted for little in the 2-1 League Cup loss at Dunfermline.

TUESDAY 13th AUGUST 1996

Motherwell were stunned at home in the League Cup by lowly Alloa. The hosts failed to score in 120 minutes and lost the resulting penalty shoot-out. Willie Falconer and John Philliben missed from the spot, leaving the small band of visiting fans to celebrate enthusiastically in the Main Stand.

SATURDAY 14th AUGUST 1948

Motherwell published a programme for the first time at the start of the 1948/49 season. Rangers were the opponents and early collectors were able to mark '1-1, Mathie' on the small edition which cost only 2d.

SATURDAY 14th AUGUST 1982

Jock Wallace won his first game in charge by beating Hearts 2-1 in the League Cup. Brian Coyne and Alfie Conn got the goals to secure the victory but Wallace struggled to impose himself at Fir Park and returned to his former club Rangers early in the following season.

WEDNESDAY 14th AUGUST 1991

Dutch keeper Sieb Dykstra agreed a deal and competed for the number one spot with Billy Thomson. Dykstra eventually came out on top.

SATURDAY 15TH AUGUST 1903

After election to the top division, Motherwell started their first top-flight season with a match against Airdrie. The Diamonds were also making their First Division debut and picked up a 2-1 victory on a muddy park in a game played in pouring rain.

SATURDAY 15TH AUGUST 1931

An early blow was delivered in the title race when Rangers were defeated 4-2 at Fir Park. A crowd of 25,000 saw goals from Johnny Murdoch (2), George Stevenson and Willie Dowall deliver the win. Motherwell made a brilliant start to the campaign by winning the first three games to open an early lead in the championship.

SATURDAY 15TH AUGUST 1959

Motherwell won an astonishing League Cup tie 3-1 at Easter Road thanks to a remarkable hat-trick from Ian St John. The striker's 2½ minute treble was the quickest ever in British football.

TUESDAY 15TH AUGUST 1989

Having been suspended in the league, Davie Cooper made his Motherwell debut at Rugby Park in the League Cup. Kilmarnock had no answer for his skill as pinpoint crosses set up two goals for Nick Cusack in an easy 4-1 win.

WEDNESDAY 16TH AUGUST 1911

Sailor Hunter was in charge for the first time, as a goal from Davie Lindley secured a 1-1 draw away to Queen's Park.

THURSDAY 17TH AUGUST 1995

Lee McCulloch signed from Cumbernauld United on this day in 1995. It took him some time to find the net – the striker made over 30 appearances before breaking his scoring duck against Hibs in 1998.

TUESDAY 18TH AUGUST 1998

John Boyle took over the club in a £2.5m deal from John Chapman and his family. Boyle initially stated he would maintain strict financial discipline but was soon backing a huge spending campaign in a bid to turn the club into the third force in Scottish football.

LEE McCULLOCH LINES UP FOR SCOTLAND

SATURDAY 19TH AUGUST 1916

Hugh Ferguson made his debut in a wartime league game against Raith Rovers. The newcomer instantly bagged two goals in a 2-2 draw and a hat-trick against Dundee helped him to an early record of seven goals in as many games. Ferguson would go on to become the club's record goalscorer before being sold to Cardiff City.

SATURDAY 19TH AUGUST 1995

Motherwell were taken to penalties in a League Cup clash in their last ever visit to Clydebank but many fans will remember the appearance of goalkeeper Stevie Woods as a late substitute on the right wing. Injury prompted the move and Woods battled away without disgracing himself. Woods saw off several challenging goalkeepers during his nine years at Fir Park but his ability to follow up wonderful saves with diabolical mistakes frustrated the Motherwell support.

SATURDAY 20TH AUGUST 2005

Dundee United came to Fir Park and stole a remarkable 5-4 victory. Motherwell led by 2-0, 3-1 and 4-2 before a collapse saw the match slip away. The hosts could still have secured a draw but were denied a very strong penalty claim in the last minute.

SATURDAY 21ST AUGUST 1968

Tom Forsyth made his Motherwell debut in the Second Division defeat of Albion Rovers. Forsyth was normally used as a forward at Fir Park and was a strong member of the side which re-established itself in the top flight. International honours and a transfer to Rangers followed where he famously scored a winning goal from six inches in the cup final. He returned to Fir Park as assistant manager in 1984 but moved to Hearts with Tommy McLean.

SATURDAY 21ST AUGUST 1993

Motherwell moved to the top of the league thanks to a 1-0 victory at Rugby Park. Paul McGrillen grabbed the only goal as the side made a positive start to what would be a successful campaign.

SATURDAY 22ND AUGUST 1981

Ally McLeod tried to improve the squad before the start of the new season but despite the new arrivals the League Cup campaign was dismal. McLeod left after a 1-0 defeat at home to Partick Thistle and Davie Hay was promoted from his role as assistant to take over in the manager's chair.

TUESDAY 22ND AUGUST 1995

Motherwell were trying to become the first Scottish club ever to progress in Europe having lost the first leg at home. Dougie Arnott and Alex Burns secured a 2-0 win away to MyPa but this wasn't enough to overcome the 3-1 deficit. Glory was almost secured when Lee McCulloch's shot grazed the post in injury time.

WEDNESDAY 23RD AUGUST 1913

New colours were worn for the first time when Celtic came to visit Fir Park. A 1-1 draw was secured thanks to a goal from Robert Spiers but the claret and amber shirts worn by the side proved much more memorable. Blue and white was ditched and though it has been suggested the Duke of Hamilton's racing colours were copied, it is more likely Bradford's FA Cup win in 1912 inspired the change.

SATURDAY 23RD AUGUST 1986

Steve Kirk made the first of 301 league appearances for Motherwell in a 0-0 draw against Hibs. Kirk would go on to score 63 league goals and more in the cups, most notably in the winning run of 1991.

TUESDAY 23RD AUGUST 1994

The Uefa Cup campaign continued as Havnar Bóltfelag were swept away 4-1 in the Faroe Islands. Motherwell were the first Scottish side to lose a goal to a team from the Islands but strikes from Steve Kirk (2), Alex Burns and Billy Davies made that irrelevant. Ray Allan made his only competitive appearance in goals from the bench, giving him the rare distinction of having not played in the Scottish top flight but in the highest level of European competition.

SUNDAY 24TH AUGUST 1958

Legendary winger Johnny Gahagan was born in Glasgow in 1958. He was very popular with the fans in his ten-year spell at Fir Park, but one record he won't be overly proud of is that he made more Motherwell substitute appearances than anyone else – 93!

WEDNESDAY 24TH AUGUST 1960

There was a new look to Fir Park as Motherwell took on Ayr United. Floodlight pylons replaced the old system but the match was also notable for the appearance of three Weirs in the team; Hastie in goal, Andy on the left wing and Ian at left-back.

FRIDAY 24TH AUGUST 1984

Tommy Boyd finally collected his Player of the Year prize from Trust Motors for his efforts the previous season. He received a car for a year but the presentation was delayed until he had passed his driving test in the middle of the month.

SATURDAY 24TH AUGUST 1996

After two draws to start the season, Motherwell got their first win on the board at Raith Rovers. Two goals from Mitchell van der Gaag, with one in between from Dougie Arnott, gave the visitors a comfortable 3-0 victory.

WEDNESDAY 25TH AUGUST 1981

The Motherwell board decided to terminate the contract of manager Ally McLeod. Following the League Cup loss to Partick Thistle the previous Saturday, the fifth defeat in succession, Motherwell fans had gathered outside the Main Stand to protest against the manager – and the direct action had a near immediate effect.

SATURDAY 25TH AUGUST 1990

Fir Park was rocking for the opening day of the season when goals from Dougie Arnott and Bobby Russell produced a 2-0 win over Celtic. The game was also notable for an off-the-ball incident when Colin O'Neil floored Peter Grant with his elbow. After the incident was seen on television, he was banned for eight games, allegedly on the say-so of the fourth official.

SATURDAY 26TH AUGUST 1939

George Stevenson made the last of his 510 appearances for Motherwell in a game against Alloa. A 3-2 loss was not a fitting end to his career but he more than made up for that with a successful spell as manager after the war.

WEDNESDAY 26TH AUGUST 1981

Following the resignation of Ally McLeod, Davie Hay took over as manager. He inspired the team which romped through the First Division before he departed to America.

SATURDAY 27TH AUGUST 1938

A remarkable start to the season was completed when Motherwell defeated Kilmarnock 5-2 at Fir Park. Defender Ben Ellis grabbed a hat-trick of penalties as the side notched 18 goals in the opening four league games.

SATURDAY 27TH AUGUST 1994

Phil O'Donnell played what seemed like his last game for the club in a narrow win at Kilmarnock. The side were preparing for the Uefa Cup clash with Borussia Dortmund but O'Donnell was transferred to Celtic for a club record £1.75m just before the team flew to Germany. O'Donnell then moved to Sheffield Wednesday after Celtic and eventually returned to Fir Park in the middle of the 2003/04 season.

SATURDAY 28TH AUGUST 1926

Motherwell dropped points for the only time in the first four games in a 1-1 draw at Falkirk. Excellent scoring form from Willie McFadyen and Bobby Ferrier brought seven points from eight to open the season and the team eventually finished runners up... the best finish yet.

SATURDAY 28TH AUGUST 2004

Phil O'Donnell's renaissance continued as Motherwell made a positive start to the season under Terry Butcher. A Kevin McBride penalty had given 'Well the lead against Hearts before O'Donnell secured the points with a stunning volley.

SATURDAY 29TH AUGUST 1969

The 4-1 victory over Kilmarnock was watched by pupils and teachers from Motherwell's twin town Schweinfurt, in Bavaria, who had made a 30-hour bus journey to reach Scotland. The guests made a banner saying 'Schweinfurt Supports Motherwell' and backed the team vocally by singing: "Motherwell vor, noch ein Tor!"

SATURDAY 30TH AUGUST 1975

A tenth-place finish in the previous season earned Motherwell the right to take part in the first ever Premier League. Gregor Stevens got the first goal in a 1-1 draw at home to Ayr but Motherwell needed seven games to record a win after drawing five out of the first six. Willie Pettigrew certainly adapted quickly to the new league as he scored ten goals in the opening nine games. He finished with a remarkable 32 goals in all competitions, a tally unmatched since.

SATURDAY 30TH AUGUST 2003

Motherwell said farewell to James McFadden in a 2-2 draw with Partick Thistle. Faddy left more fond memories by scoring both goals, the first of which was a stunning drive from 25 yards. He moved to Everton for £1.25m after scoring 32 goals in 70 appearances.

WEDNESDAY 31ST AUGUST 1994

A great chance was missed when Airdrie defeated Motherwell in the League Cup. Motherwell had an excellent side at this time but the local rivals came out on top in the last meeting between the teams thanks to an extra-time winner.

SUNDAY 31ST AUGUST 2003

Fans hoped the transfer window would pass without someone swooping for James McFadden but in the closing hours Everton completed a deal for the striker. While there was initially disappointment, the team flourished without him and the club was able to use the transfer fee as the basis for coming out of administration. A sell-on clause was included in the deal so Motherwell received more money in 2008 when he moved to Birmingham City.

MOTHERWELL FC
On This Day

SEPTEMBER

WEDNESDAY 1st SEPTEMBER 1954

A 1-0 win at Rugby Park was enough to lift Motherwell out of the League Cup group stage for the first time in three years. Just as with the last occasion, the side capitalised in the knockout phases and made it all the way to the final at Hampden.

SATURDAY 2nd SEPTEMBER 1933

After the disappointment of failing to retain the title the previous season, Motherwell tried to regain the championship. The first four matches were all won and when a Willie McFadyen double brought a 2-1 victory over Rangers, an early lead had been established. Motherwell went on to win the first nine games of the season and did not lose until just before Christmas.

SATURDAY 2nd SEPTEMBER 1939

Any lingering chance Motherwell had of returning to the glory days of the early 1930s disappeared with the start of the Second World War. Hugh Wales and John McCulloch scored the last peacetime goals in the defeat to Hearts on this day.

SATURDAY 2nd SEPTEMBER 1950

A 3-2 win at Firhill was enough to secure Motherwell's passage from the group stages of the League Cup. Partick Thistle, Airdrie and Hearts had been seen off which meant Motherwell had qualified for the quarter-finals for the first time.

SATURDAY 2nd SEPTEMBER 1978

Having lost 3-1 to Clyde at Shawfield in a League Cup first-leg, Motherwell had it all to do in the Fir Park return. A crowd of 3,803 saw goals from Willie Pettigrew, Peter Marinello and Ian Clinging complete a superb comeback and set up a tie with Celtic.

THURSDAY 3rd SEPTEMBER 1998

Pat Nevin signed from Kilmarnock but not just as an ordinary player. John Boyle wanted him to run the club for him so in addition he took on the role of chief executive. Nevin was nearing the end of his playing days but still contributed well before retiring to concentrate on working behind the scenes.

SATURDAY 4TH SEPTEMBER 1982

After failing to progress from the League Cup group, Jock Wallace had his first league game at Fir Park against former club Rangers. He was given a massive ovation by the visiting support and acknowledged them more than his new fans. Rangers raced into a two goal lead but goals from Bruce Cleland and Joe Carson secured a 2-2 draw.

WEDNESDAY 4TH SEPTEMBER 1991

The League Cup campaign came to an end at Tannadice with a 2-0 loss to Dundee United. Morton and Clyde had been dispatched in previous rounds but the Terrors proved too strong in the quarter-final. Revenge would be had against United later in the season...

SATURDAY 4TH SEPTEMBER 1993

With the side setting pretty at the top of the league, a large support travelled to McDiarmid Park. As often happens when expectation is raised, disappointment followed in the shape of a 3-0 loss. The match was not nearly as clear-cut as the result suggested, but the hosts took their chances while Motherwell did not.

SATURDAY 5TH SEPTEMBER 1959

The first home game of the season was played against Airdrie in the new look Fir Park. Concrete steps had been built under the covered enclosure, and on parts of the terracing, to improve spectator comfort. The capacity was now increased to 40,000. Only 13,423 were in the ground, though, as a Pat Quinn hat-trick and another from Ian St John brought a 4-1 victory.

WEDNESDAY 6TH SEPTEMBER 2006

Stephen Craigan played a crucial role in the centre of defence as Northern Ireland triumphed 3-2 over Spain. The Motherwell defender matched up against the likes of Torres, Villa and Raul as his country recorded a famous victory. Northern Ireland's campaign also included a great home win over Sweden but they came up just short of qualifying for the finals. Craigan is now Motherwell's most capped player with over 30 international appearances.

SATURDAY 7TH SEPTEMBER 1929

Motherwell slumped to a 2-0 home defeat by Hearts but little did anyone realise it would be the last home loss for some time. The side became consistent challengers at the top of the Scottish league and stayed unbeaten at Fir Park until October 1932.

SATURDAY 7TH SEPTEMBER 1968

Forfar Athletic defeated Motherwell 1-0 at Station Park in the Second Division. However, the side didn't take long to adapt to their new surroundings in the lower league and promptly stormed their way to promotion. This was the last defeat until February, 21 games later.

TUESDAY 7TH SEPTEMBER 1993

Paul Lambert joined the squad for the first time after Tommy McLean bought him from St Mirren in a £250,000 deal. Lambert boosted the midfield playing over 100 games for the club before moving to Borussia Dortmund with whom he won the Champions League.

SATURDAY 8TH SEPTEMBER 1951

Much work was done at Fir Park over the summer as a new façade and turnstiles were built along with rooms for the manager and secretary. There were new facilities for entertaining opposing directors, which were enjoyed for the first time by Celtic officials on this day.

WEDNESDAY 9TH SEPTEMBER 1953

Local junior side Bellshill Athletic opened their new Brandon Park with a glamour game. However, they stood aside as Motherwell and Third Lanark played an exhibition which Thirds won 4-1.

FRIDAY 9TH SEPTEMBER 1994

Phil O'Donnell was transferred to Celtic for a record fee of £1.75m. Speculation surrounded the young midfielder for some time before Tommy Burns finally made an offer which couldn't be refused. O'Donnell won the title and cup at Parkhead before moving to Sheffield Wednesday on a free.

TUESDAY 9TH SEPTEMBER 1997

Franz Resch and Mario Dorner were freed by boss Alex McLeish. The big summer signings from VfB Modling were disappointments and were released to continue their careers in England.

SATURDAY 10TH SEPTEMBER 1955

After successfully negotiating the League Cup group phase, Bobby Ancell faced East Fife in his first league game as Motherwell manager. It went well with the Fifers losing 5-2 thanks to a hat-trick from Johnny Aitkenhead and singles from Billy Reid and Alex Bain.

TUESDAY 10TH SEPTEMBER 2002

Motherwell's young side were given little chance against Celtic but recorded the first famous win of the administration period at Fir Park. Henrik Larsson missed several good chances in the first half before a Shaun Fagan diving header opened the scoring late in the game. A penalty by James McFadden turned out to be the winner as Maloney scored a last minute consolation goal.

SATURDAY 11TH SEPTEMBER 1886

Motherwell entered the Scottish Cup for first time but things went badly: Cambuslang defeated them 6-1.

SATURDAY 11TH SEPTEMBER 1954

The big time returned to Fir Park when Motherwell faced Falkirk in the First Division. They had cruised to promotion in the previous season and began the new season with a 1-1 draw; Charlie Cox got the goal.

SATURDAY 12TH SEPTEMBER 1931

The title charge continued with a convincing 4-1 home victory over Falkirk. Bobby Ferrier, Tom Douglas, Willie McFadyen and George Stevenson provided the goals as Motherwell continued to slug it out with Rangers at the top of the table.

SATURDAY 12TH SEPTEMBER 1936

The 3-2 defeat at Rangers was the beginning of the end for goalkeeping legend Alan McClory. He had been signed in 1924 as a replacement for Jock Rundell and contributed hugely to the title win in 1932.

TUESDAY 13TH SEPTEMBER 1994

Motherwell travelled to Borussia Dortmund in the first round of the Uefa Cup. On paper the Steelmen had little chance against the Bundesliga stars but an excellent performance gave the hosts a fright. Several chances were missed but the only goal of the match came from Andreas Möller in the second half.

MONDAY 14TH SEPTEMBER 1970

Pele couldn't beat Gordon Banks at the 1970 World Cup but John Goldthorp had no such problem. He got the only goal of the game as Stoke City were defeated 1-0 at Fir Park in the Texaco Cup.

SATURDAY 14TH SEPTEMBER 1974

Ian St John's last game in charge was a 4-0 win at Ayr United. He moved to Portsmouth, which he later admitted was a mistake, but in difficult circumstances he couldn't do a good job. Pompey offered Peter Marinello in lieu of compensation.

SUNDAY 15TH SEPTEMBER 2002

It is not possible to be relegated in September but Motherwell came pretty close in 2002. The team collapsed in spectacular fashion at Tynecastle, throwing away a two-goal lead on the way to a 4-2 loss. This started a run of just one point from a possible 33 which resulted in a fall from the middle of the table to the bottom.

SATURDAY 16TH SEPTEMBER 1950

After making the quarter-finals of the League Cup for the first time, Motherwell showed no signs of stopping. Celtic were humbled 4-1 at Parkhead thanks to an own goal and strikes from Jimmy Watson, Jim Forrest and Jackie Hunter. There was still business to take care of in the second leg and despite losing 1-0 Motherwell went through to the semi-final against Ayr United.

SUNDAY 16TH SEPTEMBER 2001

A dreadful start to the season cost Billy Davies his job. A 3-0 loss at Ibrox meant only three points had been collected from seven matches and Davies paid the price a few days later.

WEDNESDAY 17TH SEPTEMBER 2003

Bryan Jackson announced that the club could begin the process of leaving administration. Improved financial stability and the proceeds from the sale of James McFadden made the move possible. Creditors received some of the money due to them as John Boyle wrote off several million pounds owed to him personally.

SATURDAY 17TH SEPTEMBER 2005

After two successive top six finishes, Motherwell looked to enjoy another strong season. Newly promoted Falkirk were beaten 5-0 at Fir Park with goals coming from Jim Hamilton, Richie Foran (2), Scott McDonald and Shaun Fagan.

WEDNESDAY 18TH SEPTEMBER 1991

Motherwell made their European debut in the Cup Winners' Cup away to Katowice in Poland. Several hundred fans made the journey, including a bus-load who saw only the closing minutes after being held up on the way. Motherwell performed respectably but went down to a 2-0 defeat.

TUESDAY 18TH SEPTEMBER 2001

Billy Davies was sacked due to the season's poor start. Davies had originally saved the side from relegation when he took over in 1998 and the team finished fourth under his guidance the following year. Financial cuts made life difficult in the months to come and Davies struggled to rebuild the side with a smaller budget.

SATURDAY 18TH SEPTEMBER 2004

Alex Burns' last goal in a Motherwell jersey capped an excellent 4-2 victory over Dundee United. Burns returned to Motherwell from Partick Thistle in 2003 but struggled to score, hitting only five goals in 47 games.

SATURDAY 19TH SEPTEMBER 1992

Even the best managers make mistakes and Tommy McLean will reflect that the signing of Paul Baker was not his most inspired move. Baker's only goal came in this 3-3 draw at home to St Johnstone.

MONDAY 20TH SEPTEMBER 1999

Motherwell were leading Hearts 1-0 at half-time when the game was abandoned due to a waterlogged pitch. Shaun Teale's penalty had put the hosts in front but referee John Rowbotham decided the game couldn't go on and called a halt at the break. Chairman John Boyle was particularly outraged when it was discovered Hearts' chief executive Chris Robinson had visited the referee at half-time to discuss the safety of the players on the pitch.

SATURDAY 21ST SEPTEMBER 1946

The first official League Cup competition was played in 1946 but Motherwell started with a loss at home to Queen of the South. Despite two wins over Aberdeen and another victory against Falkirk, Motherwell were unable to escape the group stage and reach the quarter-finals.

SATURDAY 21ST SEPTEMBER 1985

Tommy McLean's side took some time to adjust to the Premier League and needed seven games before the first victory was recorded. The 2-1 success over Hearts was also notable since a bomb warning was phoned in to the vice president's club and the police insisted on evacuating the covered enclosure. No package was found and after an 11-minute delay the second half was allowed to proceed.

SATURDAY 22ND SEPTEMBER 1956

Bobby Ancell wasted no time in building a winning side. In just his second season the team hit the top of the table when Airdrie were defeated 4-1 in a Fir Park derby. Doubles from both Ian Gardiner and Bert McCann secured the win as Motherwell made a wonderful start to the campaign and would go on to challenge for the title for the first time since the 1930s.

SATURDAY 22ND SEPTEMBER 2001

John Philliben and Miodrag Krivokapic took over following the dismissal of Billy Davies and instantly inspired the team to a win over Hearts. A stunning first goal from David Kelly and a header from Stuart Elliot earned a 2-0 victory.

MONDAY 23rd SEPTEMBER 1918

The board deemed that James Archibald had been a non-trier in a previous game and resolved to sack him after four weeks' notice had been given. Archibald survived a little longer at Fir Park but was sold to Spurs for £100 in 1919.

SATURDAY 23rd SEPTEMBER 1967

John Goldthorp made his debut for Motherwell in a 1-1 draw with Dunfermline. The big striker was used sparingly following his capture from Lesmahagow Juniors but Goldie became a fixture in the Fir Park side over the years.

TUESDAY 23rd SEPTEMBER 1986

Motherwell hoped to reach their first League Cup final in 32 years but looked down and out when two goals gave Celtic a comfortable lead in the Hampden semi-final. Strikes from Andy Walker and Paul Smith took the game to extra time followed by a penalty shoot-out. Everyone found the net with the exception of poor John Philliben, who smacked the bar.

WEDNESDAY 23rd SEPTEMBER 1987

A year to the day after Motherwell lost to Celtic in the League Cup semi-final, the side came up short at Hampden against the other half of the Old Firm. Paul Smith had given Motherwell the lead but things fell apart shortly before half-time with Steve Kirk putting through his own goal and John Fleck scoring. The game was lost when Mark Falco clinched it in the closing minutes.

SATURDAY 24th SEPTEMBER 1927

The club's ever-improving performances meant that the ground had to be extended to accommodate more spectators for big games. Cart horses carried ashes to extend the banking around the pitch and 30,000 watched a dull draw with Rangers.

SATURDAY 24th SEPTEMBER 1966

One of the few players to notch five in a game for Motherwell since the Ancell era was Bobby Campbell. He grabbed all five in a 5-0 win at Falkirk on the way to becoming top scorer for the campaign.

MONDAY 25TH SEPTEMBER 1933

A remarkable start to the season, nine consecutive wins, came to an end with a 1-1 draw at Pittodrie. George Stevenson scored Motherwell's goal in the tussle with Aberdeen which was enough to keep the team sitting pretty at the top of the table.

SATURDAY 25TH SEPTEMBER 1954

Motherwell secured an excellent victory over Rangers in the quarter-finals of the League Cup. Having won 2-1 at home in the midweek first leg, the side travelled to Ibrox on the Saturday knowing a draw would be enough to progress. The match ended 1-1 and Motherwell went on to face East Fife in the semi-final.

SATURDAY 25TH SEPTEMBER 2004

Terry Butcher had the side playing good football and an enthusiastic support travelled to see the team take on Livingston. An exciting SPL match was won 3-2 and there was another boost to come later in the evening when the League Cup quarter-final draw kept Motherwell away from the Old Firm and set up another trip to Almondvale in November.

MONDAY 26TH SEPTEMBER 1960

A second game to inaugurate the Fir Park floodlights took place against Bahia of Brazil. This time the lights were mounted on pylons at the corners of the ground, replacing the roof lights on either side of the pitch. Goals from Bobby Young, Ian St John and Willie Hunter brought a 3-1 victory and heralded the start of a floodlit friendly era at Fir Park in which Motherwell faced top sides from all over the world.

TUESDAY 27TH SEPTEMBER 1994

Motherwell failed to turn around the first leg loss in Germany as they lost 2-0 to Borussia Dortmund at Fir Park. Goals in each half, coupled with red cards for Dougie Arnott and Rab Shannon, sent the team crashing out. The game was played in mid-afternoon to suit German television demands which meant many half-days were taken in a bid to see the match.

SATURDAY 28TH SEPTEMBER 1974

Following the loss of manager Ian St John to Portsmouth, Willie McLean was chosen as the replacement. He eventually turned the team into one of the better sides in Scotland but his first game in charge was a 1-0 loss to Dundee at Dens Park.

SATURDAY 29TH SEPTEMBER 2001

The temporary duo in charge, John Philliben and Miodrag Krivokapic, would both be overlooked when the full-time position was appointed. However, they did lead the team to one of the most vital wins of the season at St Johnstone. The Saints were leading 2-1 with only 15 minutes to go when Stuart Elliot equalised and then Stephen Nicholas grabbed a last minute winner. Rather than the clubs being level on points, Motherwell opened up a six-point gap above the relegation zone.

MONDAY 30TH SEPTEMBER 1929

George Stevenson enjoyed a benefit game against Huddersfield Town. Admission was 1/- for the early evening kick-off which the visitors won 4-2 despite a double from Bobby Ferrier. The visitors were one of the most successful sides in England at the time having won three championships and an FA Cup earlier in the decade.

TUESDAY 30TH SEPTEMBER 1969

Motherwell reached the League Cup semi-final with an epic quarter-final win over Morton. The first leg was lost 3-0 at Cappielow and a sensational return at Fir Park brought an equally convincing 3-0 win for Motherwell. That meant a replay at neutral Ibrox and Jumbo Muir's late goal was enough to send the 'Well to Hampden.

WEDNESDAY 30TH SEPTEMBER 1970

A 2-1 defeat at Stoke in the Texaco Cup meant that extra time and penalties were needed to separate the teams. 'Dixie' Deans missed for Motherwell but successful strikes from Davie Whiteford, Jackie McInally, Brian Heron and John Goldthorp put the pressure on Stoke. Goalkeeper Keith McCrae saved two Stoke kicks and was carried shoulder high from the field by his jubilant teammates.

MOTHERWELL FC
On This Day

OCTOBER

SATURDAY 1st OCTOBER 1955

Motherwell looked to return to the League Cup final for the second season in a row when they faced St Mirren in the semi-final at Ibrox. A period of extra time could not separate the sides after an enthralling 3-3 draw.

FRIDAY 1st OCTOBER 1982

Willie Irvine was a prolific scorer but chose to move on to bigger things. He went to Hibs in exchange for Bobby Flavell and did well at Easter Road, becoming the Premier League top scorer in 1983/84. Flavell was not as successful at Fir Park but did chip in a few goals.

FRIDAY 2nd OCTOBER 1953

William Pettigrew was born in Motherwell on this day in 1953. Willie started his career at Hibs but failed to play for the first team before moving to East Kilbride Thistle. Motherwell snapped him up and he scored dozens of goals before going to Dundee United where he won two League Cup medals. A First Division title with Hearts followed before spells at Morton and Hamilton ended his career.

WEDNESDAY 2nd OCTOBER 1991

Over 10,000 watched Katowice in the Cup Winners' Cup second leg at Fir Park. Motherwell trailed 2-0 from the first game and hoped to cause an upset. Dariusz Rzezniczek's equaliser in the second-half effectively ended the contest although late strikes from Nick Cusack and Steve Kirk secured a victory on the night.

SATURDAY 3rd OCTOBER 1903

Motherwell recorded their first ever win in the top flight. Partick Thistle were defeated 2-0 at Fir Park but the 'Well struggled, winning only six out of 26 games, at the higher level and finished second-bottom.

TUESDAY 3rd OCTOBER 1989

Davie Cooper and Bobby Russell combined to score the only goal against their former club, Rangers, in a midweek clash at Fir Park. The 1-0 win sent the team to the top of the league for the first time in several years.

WEDNESDAY 4TH OCTOBER 1978

After a dramatic win over Clyde in the previous round, Motherwell travelled to Celtic for the first leg of a League Cup clash. Willie Pettigrew grabbed the only goal of the game to give Motherwell a vital lead but things went horribly wrong in the second leg. Celtic triumphed 4-1 at Fir Park to send Motherwell crashing out of the cup once again.

SATURDAY 5TH OCTOBER 1985

The programme for the match against Rangers carried an advertisement for Motherwell's new cheerleading team. A small notice invited 'young ladies' aged 16-60 to apply by contacting the club.

SATURDAY 6TH OCTOBER 1923

After two straight losses Motherwell went on an eight-game unbeaten run. One of these games was a dull 0-0 draw at Ayr which was mainly notable for the debut of Willie McFadyen at outside right. McFadyen would eventually establish himself as a free-scoring centre-forward, bagging a record 52 goals in the championship year of 1932.

SATURDAY 7TH OCTOBER 1950

After a two-leg win over Celtic, Motherwell faced Ayr United in the League Cup semi-final and advanced after a thrilling 90 minutes. Ayr led but goals from Johnny Aitkenhead and Jimmy Watson put 'Well in front. Then Ayr turned the tie on its head, grabbing two goals, and looked to be going through with only six minutes to go. But, Aitkenhead equalised and when Watson scored the winner Motherwell had done enough to meet Hibs in the Hampden final.

THURSDAY 7TH OCTOBER 1982

Jock Wallace added Ally Mauchlen to the squad as he tried to guide the team to Premier League survival. Mauchlen was a tough-tackling midfielder but developed admirable leadership qualities and was influential in helping the side to promotion back to the top flight in 1985. Leicester City were then made aware of his talent and snapped him up along with Gary McAllister in a combined deal worth £250,000.

SATURDAY 8TH OCTOBER 1988

Cult hero Steve Kirk is best known for his scoring ability and also as an emergency goalkeeper. After Cammy Duncan was injured at Tynecastle, Kirk stepped between the posts and saved a penalty kick from Wayne Foster. That helped the side to a 2-2 draw with Ray Farningham and Craig Paterson getting the goals.

SATURDAY 8TH OCTOBER 1994

Motherwell started a winning run of five games with a remarkable 5-3 victory over Falkirk. The Bairns fought back from two down to lead 3-2 before Motherwell rallied late on to claim a wonderful victory. Tommy Coyne scored twice but could have had more as Tony Parks saved two penalties from the striker.

FRIDAY 8TH OCTOBER 1999

Motherwell travelled to Airdrie's new ground for the first time as official guests for the glamour opening. Goals from Derek Townsley and Stephen Halliday gave the visitors a simple 2-0 win.

THURSDAY 9TH OCTOBER 1947

On this day Joe Wark was born in Glasgow. He spent his entire senior career at Motherwell having signed from Irvine Vics and holds the post-war appearance record with 469 in the league. Despite playing in several semi-finals, major honours eluded him and there still remains a strong conviction among Motherwell fans that Wark was the best player never to have received a full Scotland cap.

SATURDAY 9TH OCTOBER 1954

Motherwell reached their fourth final of the 1950s by defeating holders East Fife 2-1 in a Hampden Park semi-final. The Fifers had taken an early lead but Willie Kilmarnock's free-kick levelled things and Alex Bain grabbed the winner.

SATURDAY 9TH OCTOBER 1982

As the side battled relegation, a rare 2-0 win was recorded against St Mirren. New signing Bobby Flavell scored a stunning 35-yard goal on his debut. Sadly Flavell would only contribute another five league goals before moving to Dundee United on a free transfer.

WEDNESDAY 10TH OCTOBER 1973

After losing to Celtic at Fir Park in the first leg of the League Cup, the side produced a memorable win at Parkhead to force a decisive third game. John Goldthorp's goal and Keith McCrae's penalty save ensured an aggregate draw. Motherwell lost the replay.

SATURDAY 11TH OCTOBER 1975

The first win in the new-look Premier League finally arrived at the seventh time of asking. Goals from Willie Pettigrew and Gregor Stevens brought a 2-1 win over Hibs after five draws and one defeat.

SUNDAY 11TH OCTOBER 1981

The San Jose Earthquakes visited Fir Park for a friendly George Best was in the twilight of his career and played for the American team in the match before switching to Motherwell at half-time as the Steelmen won 5-2.

FRIDAY 11TH OCTOBER 1996

Long-serving chairman John Chapman announced he was selling his 51 per cent in the club and retiring from all business interests. Chapman had been on the board since 1981 and in the chair since 1987.

SUNDAY 11TH OCTOBER 1998

As part of the £400,000 deal which took Mitchell van der Gaag back to Holland with FC Utrecht, Motherwell travelled to play his new side in a friendly. Utrecht won 4-1, but afterwards Harri Kampman flew directly from Schipol to Helsinki and resigned a few days later.

THURSDAY 12TH OCTOBER 1972

The day after Tom Forsyth was sold to Rangers, manager Bobby Howitt travelled south to negotiate with Crystal Palace about Sam Goodwin. Goodwin signed the next day and made his debut against Forsyth on Saturday when Motherwell lost 2-0 to Rangers.

WEDNESDAY 12TH OCTOBER 1977

The Civil Aviation Authority blocked a plan by Barratt Homes to land a helicopter in Fir Park before the forthcoming game with Rangers. The stunt was designed to promote their sponsorship of the match.

SATURDAY 13th OCTOBER 1951

The defence of the League Cup ended with a heavy loss to Dundee in the semi-final at Hampden. A tremendous performance from the Dark Blues produced a 5-1 win with a Flavell hat-trick doing most of the damage. Motherwell's consolation was scored by Jim Forrest but revenge would come against Dundee later in the season.

WEDNESDAY 13th OCTOBER 1999

Motherwell travelled to the Caledonian Stadium to take on Inverness in the League Cup third round. A firm header from Lee McCulloch – after good work from Pat Nevin – was enough to win the tie.

SATURDAY 14th OCTOBER 1967

Stirling Albion were defeated 3-1 at Fir Park but this turned out to be the only win of the season before Christmas. Clyde were finally beaten to end the run but by then the side were deep in relegation trouble with only the woeful Binos below them in the table.

SATURDAY 14th OCTOBER 1995

Goals from Tommy Coyne and Paul Lambert secured a 2-1 victory at home despite losing the first goal to Aberdeen. A major goal scoring problem then struck and this would be the last victory for fifteen games as the team became embroiled in a relegation battle with Falkirk and Partick Thistle.

WEDNESDAY 14th OCTOBER 1998

After weeks of speculation, Harri Kampman resigned as manager. The amiable Finn left with a dismal record after his time at Fir Park and the side was hovering just above the relegation zone. Veteran midfielder Billy Davies was appointed later the same day and immediately announced he would end his playing career to concentrate on management.

SATURDAY 14th OCTOBER 2000

In a match which was a lot more even than the score suggested, Motherwell triumphed 4-0 over St Johnstone. Luck was on the side of the hosts as an own goal and a penalty from Brannan smoothed the way to victory.

SATURDAY 15TH OCTOBER 1949

A dismal start to the season produced only three points from five games. The first win eventually came against Partick Thistle thanks to goals from Willie McCall and Wilson Humphries but it would be the only victory until mid-November.

SATURDAY 15TH OCTOBER 1960

Third Lanark went out of business in 1967 but they were still a force just a few years before. Goals from Pat Quinn (2), Ian St John and Jimmy Lindsay were not enough to stop Thirds winning 5-4 in a sensational Fir Park contest.

SATURDAY 16TH OCTOBER 1999

Summer signing Kevin Twaddle finally made his debut for the club after recovering from glandular fever. Twaddle eventually blossomed, scoring several useful goals, but a perception remained with some of the fans that he could have contributed more.

TUESDAY 16TH OCTOBER 2001

Despite John Philliben and Miodrag Krivokapic doing a solid job as temporary managers, the full-time position was given to Eric Black following the departure of Billy Davies. It was Black's first managerial position but he was a highly-rated coach and the appointment was met with optimism from the Motherwell support. Terry Butcher was to be his assistant.

SATURDAY 17TH OCTOBER 1981

The fight to get back into the Premier League was well under way and the side's excellent form continued with a convincing 7-1 win at Kilbowie. Stuart Rafferty (2), Willie Irvine (2), Chic McClelland, Johnny Gahagan and an own goal proved way too much for Clydebank.

SATURDAY 17TH OCTOBER 1998

New manager Billy Davies quickly realised the scale of the problem he faced when the side lost 5-0 at St Johnstone in his first game. A 40-yard chip from George O'Boyle was the pick of the goals.

SATURDAY 18TH OCTOBER 1930

Airdrie had finished runners-up four times in the 1920s but Motherwell had taken over as the new top dogs in Lanarkshire. The change of status was confirmed by a fantastic 5-0 win at Broomfield with goals from Johnny Murdoch (2), John McMenemy (2) and Bobby Ferrier putting the Diamonds to the sword.

SATURDAY 19TH OCTOBER 1929

Falkirk were beaten 4-3 at Fir Park but Motherwell had made an indifferent start to the season. Results continued to be mixed but an impressive nine-game winning run to end the year brought another runners-up spot.

MONDAY 20TH OCTOBER 1958

The Ancell Babes showed their flair when they dismantled Leeds United 7-0 in a floodlit friendly. Leeds were in the lower part of the table in the English First Division and stood no chance against a rampant Motherwell side. Sammy Reid, Andy Weir and Ian St John were all amongst the goalscorers.

SATURDAY 20TH OCTOBER 1973

Following the sale of goalkeeper Keith McCrae to Manchester City, a new number one was needed. Stuart Rennie took over and became one of the best keepers in the club's history. His debut was not to contain many fond memories though as the team lost 1-0 to Ayr United at Somerset Park.

WEDNESDAY 20TH OCTOBER 1999

Aberdeen were still without a win in the league and had scored only two goals when they travelled to Fir Park. With two of Scotland's best-ever keepers on show at either end – Andy Goram and Jim Leighton – no-one expected the extraordinary 11-goal thriller that followed. Aberdeen went two up and although John Spencer got one back, they were soon leading 4-1. Don Goodman scored before half-time but when Aberdeen went 5-2 and then 6-3 in front, there seemed to be no hope. Spencer completed his hat-trick and Shaun Teale's penalty brought Motherwell within one goal but despite a frantic late push no equaliser could be found.

HUNTER, WEIR, MARTIS AND ST JOHN: FOUR OF THE ANCELL BABES REPRESENTING SCOTLAND UNDER-23s

WEDNESDAY 21st OCTOBER 1970

After the penalty shoot-out win over Stoke City, it was the mighty Tottenham Hotspur up next at White Hart Lane in the Texaco Cup. The Spurs side was packed full of international stars but goals from Tom Donnelly and Jackie McInally gave Motherwell an outside chance in the second leg as they returned home with a 3-2 defeat.

TUESDAY 21st OCTOBER 1975

Motherwell were back in London for another Texaco Cup tie and this time they went one better. Willie Pettigrew's goal was enough to secure a 1-1 draw with Fulham at Craven Cottage.

SATURDAY 21st OCTOBER 1978

The team had made a dismal start to the season but after a win against Morton hopes were high for the trip to Firhill. Controversially, striker Willie Pettigrew was dropped despite scoring in the previous match, but the move did not pay dividends as 'Well lost 2-0.

SATURDAY 21st OCTOBER 1989

Davie Cooper was renowned as a penalty expert when he came to Motherwell and soon showed he had lost none of his magic. Cooper himself produced a wonderful bit of skill to win a spot-kick against Dundee United and converted it by ramming the ball into the bottom corner. He later set up the winning goal for Dougie Arnott in a 3-2 victory.

MONDAY 21st OCTOBER 1996

Alex McLeish announced he would stay at Fir Park after Hibs were refused permission to speak to him. Rather than taking the traditional option of resigning and leaving against the board's wishes, he repeated his enthusiasm for his work at Motherwell and claimed he wanted to win the title with the club.

SATURDAY 21st OCTOBER 2000

World Cup star Claudia Caniggia made his home debut for Dundee and scored a delightful chip against Motherwell. However, two headed goals from Stuart Elliot in the first five minutes had put the visitors ahead and Motherwell held on.

FRIDAY 22nd OCTOBER 1971

Mitchell van der Gaag was born in Zutphen in the Netherlands. He became the club's record signing in 1995 when Alex McLeish paid £400,000 to PSV Eindhoven for his services. Injury hampered his progress at Fir Park but he became a reliable player in the heart of the defence when fit. His moment of glory came when he equalised against Dunfermline Athletic to keep Motherwell in the Premier League in 1997 before he returned to Holland with Utrecht.

SATURDAY 22nd OCTOBER 1977

A goal by Gregor Stevens brought a 1-0 win over Hibs but it was a rare one for the team as they struggled to stay just above the relegation zone. Willie McLean had lost the magic from his earlier seasons – which had produced high finishes and cup semi-finals – and he was fighting to keep his job.

SATURDAY 22nd OCTOBER 1983

Without a league win all season, Motherwell travelled to Ibrox more in hope than in expectation. McCoist gave Rangers the lead but an equaliser from the spot by Andy Ritchie and a further goal by Junior Burns produced an unlikely win. Motherwell held on despite Ian McLeod being sent off in the closing stages.

SATURDAY 22nd OCTOBER 1994

Motherwell were in the middle of a five-game winning run when Rangers visited Fir Park. A magnificent volleyed assist from Tommy Coyne set up Dougie Arnott for the opener and he got a second after the break. Motherwell were coasting before a late own goal by John Philliben caused some nerves.

SATURDAY 23rd OCTOBER 1954

The team returned to Hampden Park for the League Cup Final against Hearts. An injury crisis hurt the side's chances and the loss of Archie Shaw was a severe blow. The Jambos played much better on the day and ran out worthy winners by 4-2. The 'Well goals came from Alex Bain and a Willie Redpath penalty

SATURDAY 24TH OCTOBER 1931

What had been an extremely impressive season continued with an excellent 5-1 win at Cowdenbeath. Willie McFadyen contributed another three goals to his total while Stevenson and Ferrier also got on the scoresheet. Motherwell had made strong starts to previous seasons though and no one was taking anything for granted about how the year would progress.

SATURDAY 25TH OCTOBER 1975

After a distinctly average start to the season Motherwell soon picked up their form. A sensational match at Dundee brought two points with a great 6-3 win. The goals came from Willie Pettigrew, who grabbed four, while Ian Taylor scored the other pair. A crowd of 6,583 witnessed the nine goals.

SATURDAY 25TH OCTOBER 1997

A dramatic injury-time winner gave Aberdeen a 2-1 victory at Fir Park despite Billy Davies' second-half equaliser. However, there would be trouble to follow as an enraged fan sprinted from the Cooper Stand to attack visiting goalkeeper Jim Leighton. Thankfully, the player was not badly hurt and the offender was immediately banned from Fir Park for life.

SATURDAY 26TH OCTOBER 1957

The Ancell Babes dished out some beatings but things occasionally went wrong. Falkirk triumphed 5-2 at Fir Park in Ian St John's debut game. St John did not score his opening goal but he did enough to keep his place for the next game when he grabbed a double against Hearts. He then notched his first hat-trick in only his fifth appearance when Queen of the South were defeated 4-2.

MONDAY 26TH OCTOBER 1998

John Boyle instantly backed new manager Billy Davies by making two major moves in the transfer market. Ged Brannan arrived from Manchester City for £378,000 and John Spencer came on loan from Everton before making the move permanent in January. Both would make an impact but as the years progressed Motherwell fans would question the return they offered for the large wages they collected.

TUESDAY 27TH OCTOBER 1931

Chairman Tom Ormiston was elected as the MP for Motherwell and Wishaw. Standing for the Conservative Party, Ormiston won the seat as part of a nationwide Tory landslide but his own majority was a narrow 799 over the Labour candidate.

WEDNESDAY 27TH OCTOBER 1999

Just a week after the sensational 6-5 loss to Aberdeen, Motherwell kept a clean sheet in a win at Celtic Park. The Saturday in between saw a 2-0 win at Tannadice and when Motherwell defeated Celtic, the side began to look like a serious contender for third place. The only goal came when a wonderful pass from Stephen McMillan released Kevin Twaddle to fire high into the net and despite Shaun Teale's second-half dismissal Motherwell held on.

MONDAY 27TH OCTOBER 2003

After placing the club in administration in April, John Boyle stood down as chairman at the AGM. Bill Dickie took over for the third time while Martin Rose, then chair of the Supporters' Trust, was also added to the board.

SATURDAY 28TH OCTOBER 1950

Hibs' forward line in the 1950s was famed throughout the land but they came unstuck in the League Cup Final against Motherwell. A superb defensive performance kept out the men in green for the first half and Motherwell improved as the game progressed. Archie Kelly opened the scoring and when Jim Forrest doubled the lead two minutes later things looked good. Willie Watters' late strike put the match beyond doubt and Motherwell had won their second major trophy.

SATURDAY 28TH OCTOBER 1978

Roger Hynd had his last game in charge when St Mirren won 2-1 at Fir Park. Willie Pettigrew got the consolation for the hosts.

WEDNESDAY 28TH OCTOBER 1998

Ged Brannan and John Spencer made their debuts against Rangers and combined brilliantly to win the game. A quick free-kick from Brannan, and a sharp turn in the box from Spencer produced the only goal.

SATURDAY 29TH OCTOBER 1932

Partick Thistle recorded a 2-1 win at Fir Park to inflict Motherwell's first loss at home in the league for three years. The last away side to win at Fir Park was Hearts in autumn 1929.

SATURDAY 29TH OCTOBER 1994

Alex McLeish's men were playing good football but also had luck on their side in the 1994/95 season. Defensive lapses from Kilmarnock allowed Motherwell to win this home game 3-2 but the visitors hit the woodwork twice and had another attempt cleared off the line as the hosts recorded a very fortuitous victory.

SUNDAY 29TH OCTOBER 2000

Motherwell and Celtic battled out a 3-3 draw on a stormy night at Fir Park. Motherwell led once and were behind twice before Ged Brannan's late penalty secured a share of the points. The game was also notable for Celtic having a goal not given despite Johan Mjällby's shot appearing to cross the line before it was cleared.

SUNDAY 30TH OCTOBER 1971

John Goldthorp, Charlie Nelson and Jackie McInally represented Motherwell in a golf tournament for senior football teams held in Hamilton. The trio did more than enough to uphold the club's honour, finishing second out of ten teams. Rangers won the competition.

SATURDAY 31ST OCTOBER 1936

Future Motherwell manager Bobby Ancell made his Scotland debut at left-back in a solid 3-1 win away to Northern Ireland. He would represent his country only once more but his playing career was interrupted by World War Two. His managerial career started at Berwick and he arrived at Fir Park via Dunfermline, the team he led to promotion in his final season at East End Park.

WEDNESDAY 31ST OCTOBER 1962

Kilmarnock were an emerging force in Scottish football in the early 1960s and gave Motherwell a hiding at Rugby Park. Bobby Roberts' consolation goal counted for little in comparison to the seven notched by the home side.

MOTHERWELL FC
On This Day

NOVEMBER

SATURDAY 1st NOVEMBER 1930

After a wonderful unbeaten start to the season, Motherwell finally succumbed and were defeated in the thirteenth match. The loss came in a 2-1 reverse to Dundee at Dens Park with Willie Dowall getting the consolation goal. Motherwell were still well placed in the league but the reputation of being nearly men wouldn't be shaken off just yet – they eventually finished third behind the Old Firm.

WEDNESDAY 1st NOVEMBER 1978

Manager Roger Hynd handed his resignation to the board after a run of eight defeats in nine games. Hynd had initially moved the team away from the bottom of the league in his first months in charge but later struggled badly. When he left, after only ten months in the job, the side were stuck firmly in the relegation zone. Assistant John Haggart took over as caretaker and instantly led the side to victory at Celtic Park.

SATURDAY 1st NOVEMBER 1997

Manager Alex McLeish missed this game at St Johnstone due to a flu bug. The team struggled without him and they fell behind 4-0 in the second half before mounting a comeback. Goals from John Hendry, Owen Coyle and Billy Davies made things tense and had Tommy Coyne not missed an earlier penalty a sensational draw could have been secured.

SATURDAY 2nd NOVEMBER 1901

Motherwell would eventually finish third in Division Two in the 1901/02 season and this was the first of two good years which would help win election to the top flight. There were some bad moments on the way though with a 4-0 defeat at the now defunct St Bernard's being one of the low points of the campaign.

TUESDAY 2nd NOVEMBER 1954

It was common practice for the manager and directors to announce the team well in advance of matches, but that was not possible here. Several injuries gave reason to postpone the decision until closer to Saturday's game with Partick Thistle.

TUESDAY 3RD NOVEMBER 1942

Andy Paton impressed playing in a trial match against Celtic 'A' despite playing centre-forward. He was offered terms and then established himself in the heart of the Motherwell defence for more than a decade. In 2007 he was named the club's greatest-ever player.

TUESDAY 3RD NOVEMBER 1970

Nearly 25,000 attended Fir Park to watch Spurs defend their 3-2 lead from the Texaco Cup first leg. The match looked over when Martin Chivers opened the scoring but Brian Heron kept the tie alive with a goal before half-time. Keith McCrae made a great save before goals from Willie Watson and Tom Donnelly gave Motherwell a remarkable 5-4 aggregate victory.

MONDAY 3RD NOVEMBER 1986

Motherwell welcomed Liverpool to Fir Park to celebrate the club's centenary year. Liverpool were one of the best sides in Europe and sent a full team north including stars such as player-manager Kenny Dalglish, Alan Hansen and Ian Rush. John Wark opened the scoring but Steve Kirk later equalised in the 1-1 draw.

THURSDAY 3RD NOVEMBER 1994

Midfielder Shaun McSkimming became Motherwell's record signing when Alex McLeish paid Kilmarnock £350,000 for his services. McSkimming waited seven games before breaking into the first team and though he went on to become a solid player fans questioned whether his performances justified the large fee.

WEDNESDAY 3RD NOVEMBER 1999

Jim Griffin was sacked as assistant manager. He had been on the staff as a player and coach for 13 years but was moved on so that Miodrag Krivokapic could assist new manager Billy Davies.

TUESDAY 4TH NOVEMBER 1975

Fulham knocked Motherwell out of the Texaco Cup in a scrappy game at Fir Park. The guests won 3-2 after drawing the first leg at home. World Cup winner Bobby Moore played in defence for the Cottagers and strolled through the match with his usual class.

SATURDAY 5TH NOVEMBER 1932

Another good win gave Motherwell hope that the title could be retained – this time it was Dundee who suffered, losing 6-1 at Fir Park.

SATURDAY 5TH NOVEMBER 1966

Motherwell were beaten 5-1 at Ibrox but could take heart from the performance of debutant Davie Whiteford at right-back. Despite being a PE teacher he kept his place at Fir Park for seven years while being only a part-time footballer. A reliable penalty taker, he was included in the greatest-ever side announced in 2007.

SATURDAY 5TH NOVEMBER 1983

Jock Wallace enjoyed his last game in charge of Motherwell before returning to Rangers with a 0-0 draw at home to St Mirren. Wallace got the job despite leading Motherwell to only one win – ironically enough at Ibrox – in the league this season leaving the side firmly entrenched in the relegation battle.

SATURDAY 5TH NOVEMBER 1994

Torrential rain at Tynecastle could not stop Motherwell putting another three points on the board. A spectacular overhead kick from Dougie Arnott set up Rab Shannon's opener before Tommy Coyne tapped in the winner early in the second half.

THURSDAY 6TH NOVEMBER 1969

Having already beaten St Johnstone with ease in the league, Motherwell expected a repeat in the semi-final of the League Cup. They received a nasty shock on this occasion as the Saints were stronger. Goals from McGarry and Aitken took them into the final at Hampden.

SATURDAY 6TH NOVEMBER 1976

Motherwell enjoyed a sensational 5-4 win over Kilmarnock at Fir Park. The guests were two up at the break but a 13 minute hat-trick from Jimmy O'Rourke in the second half changed the game. Willie Pettigrew and Vic Davidson extended the lead before Killie grabbed two more of their own to set up a dramatic finale. However, goalkeeper Stuart Rennie, who had received stitches to a face wound at half-time, kept the visitors out.

SATURDAY 7TH NOVEMBER 1925

Having sold record scorer Hugh Ferguson to Cardiff, a replacement was needed. Rather than make a signing, John Hunter moved Willie McFadyen from his wide position to centre-forward against Raith Rovers and he scored two in a 5-0 win. The switch would prove inspired and McFadyen would play a crucial part in turning Motherwell into a title-challenging club.

SATURDAY 8TH NOVEMBER 1947

For a large part of his Motherwell career, Andy Paton refused to shake hands with opponents after the match. The reason being that Brown of Partick Thistle had shaken hands with him after defeat and promptly headbutted him. Andy resolved not to make the same mistake again!

SATURDAY 8TH NOVEMBER 1986

Tommy McLean frequently infuriated Rangers by sending out defensive line-ups at Ibrox. It worked perfectly on this occasion as Ray Farningham's diving header in the 88th minute secured a 1-0 win.

SATURDAY 9TH NOVEMBER 1968

Motherwell proved too strong for the Second Division and went on a seven-game run without conceding a goal while scoring 25 themselves. The highlight was the 7-0 demolition of Berwick at Fir Park.

SATURDAY 9TH NOVEMBER 1991

When Airdrie 'keeper John Martin was sent off for a professional foul which allowed Davie Cooper to equalise from the spot, Motherwell looked favourites to win this derby. But a late sucker punch gave the Diamonds victory, and a frustrated Cooper was sent off for dissent.

TUESDAY 9TH NOVEMBER 1993

An appropriate charity for Motherwell fans – the Lanarkshire Samaritans – collected before the St Johnstone game, raising £535.

TUESDAY 9TH NOVEMBER 2004

Livingston were hammered 5-0 at Almondvale in the quarter-final of the League Cup. An own goal and strikes from Richie Foran (2), Phil O'Donnell and Kenny Wright sent Motherwell into the semi-finals.

SATURDAY 10TH NOVEMBER 1956

Bobby Ancell did not need long to work his magic and soon had the team at the top of the league. In just his second season, a fantastic start culminated in a majestic 3-2 win at Ibrox, with both of Rangers' goals coming as consolations when Motherwell had already eased off the gas having led 3-0. Johnny Aitkenhead, Ian Gardiner and Pat Quinn got the goals for the visitors. The side sadly fell away late in the season but for a time it looked as though a second championship was a real possibility.

WEDNESDAY 10TH NOVEMBER 1958

Swedish side Djurgardens IF became the first non-British side to visit Fir Park and turned in an impressive performance in a 2-1 loss. Motherwell won despite trailing by a goal at half-time.

SATURDAY 11TH NOVEMBER 1972

Motherwell struggled to find consistency this season and had already been subjected to a 7-2 defeat in Aberdeen. When Celtic visited Fir Park the Glasgow side racked up another convincing win, this time 5-0, and Motherwell would endure a disappointing year spent in mid-table obscurity.

SATURDAY 11TH NOVEMBER 2001

Two goals in the last five minutes gave Motherwell a spectacular come-from-behind win at East End Park. Dunfermline looked to have the points safely in the bag but Derek Townsley found the empty net from outside the box after a goalkeeping mistake and Ged Brannan's last-gasp penalty sealed the victory.

TUESDAY 12TH NOVEMBER 1935

At a board meeting it was noted William Rodger was in a nursing home to have his appendix removed. But, the unfortunate player would receive no wages until he was fit enough to return to work!

SUNDAY 12TH NOVEMBER 1995

A handful of people watched some stars of the future play an exciting Youth Cup tie against Huntly at Fir Park. The young 'Well side progressed 5-3 on penalties following a 4-4 draw after extra time.

SATURDAY 13TH NOVEMBER 1926

John Hunter's steady hand was producing results and the side were on the verge of becoming championship challengers. St Johnstone were thrashed 5-2 at Fir Park in the middle of a seven-game winning run which propelled the side to the top of the table.

SUNDAY 14TH NOVEMBER 1982

Stephen Hughes was born in Motherwell in 1982. After spells with Rangers and Leicester, he joined his hometown club in 2007 and contributed to the side reaching Europe in his first season.

SATURDAY 15TH NOVEMBER 1975

Motherwell were hovering around third place when they defeated Celtic 2-0 in Glasgow. A Willie Pettigrew double secured the win in front of 33,000 fans and thoughts turned to the possibility of reaching European competition for the first time.

SATURDAY 15TH NOVEMBER 1997

Exactly 22 years to the day of a 2-0 victory at Parkhead, Motherwell repeated the trick. The win at title-chasing Celtic gave a huge boost in the battle against relegation. Goals from Owen Coyle and Mickey Weir ended a run of nine without a win and a losing streak of six.

SATURDAY 16TH NOVEMBER 1996

Motherwell won 4-2 at Kilmarnock. Tommy Coyne stole the headlines with his only hat-trick as a 'Well player – a majestic lob following a defensive error gave him his treble.

SATURDAY 17TH NOVEMBER 1956

Johnny Aitkenhead played his last Motherwell game in the 2-0 defeat by Raith Rovers. The winger spent seven years at Fir Park, playing 171 times in the league and winning both domestic cups.

SATURDAY 17TH NOVEMBER 1962

One Motherwell career ended as another began. Pat Quinn played his last game before moving to Blackpool while new striker Joe McBride made his debut in the 2-0 home loss to Aberdeen. Quinn was much-loved but McBride was an excellent replacement.

MONDAY 18TH NOVEMBER 1991

John Swinburne's book about the cup final victory, *'Well Worth the Wait* was released on this day. Swinburne had previously written *The History of the Steelmen* and the next volume incorporating the cup success was warmly received by fans.

SATURDAY 18TH NOVEMBER 2006

At times Maurice Malpas' side threatened to descend into farce. An injury crisis weakened the back four but that did not cut ice with the fans who witnessed Hibs win 6-1 at Fir Park. The dismal football and appalling results under Malpas did little to endear him to the Motherwell support.

TUESDAY 19TH NOVEMBER 1929

The board discussed the possibility of allowing advertising hoardings to be placed on the concrete wall circling the pitch. In a contrast to current commercialism, it was resolved to reject the proposal.

SATURDAY 19TH NOVEMBER 1949

Archie Kelly scored against Clyde on his Motherwell debut. The strong striker, signed from Aberdeen, became a prolific scorer, getting goals in both cup final victories in the early 1950s.

MONDAY 19TH NOVEMBER 1990

Motherwell star Bobby Russell opened the 'Express Burger' restaurant in Glasgow in partnership with his cousin.

SATURDAY 20TH NOVEMBER 1920

A crowd of 8,000 saw Motherwell embarrass Dumbarton at Fir Park. The hosts ran up a convincing 8-2 win over the Sons with Ferguson grabbing four goals.

SATURDAY 20TH NOVEMBER 1948

Motherwell continued to struggle after the war but one high point was the 5-1 defeat of Hibernian. The Edinburgh side were Scottish champions at the time and would finish third in 1948/49 but on this day they had little answer to goals from Joe Johnstone, Davie Mathie, Ian Goodall and Jimmy Watson (2).

SAILOR HUNTER (ON LEFT) WITH HIS FIRST TEAM – WITHIN A FEW YEARS, THE CLUB WERE TITLE CONTENDERS

SATURDAY 21st NOVEMBER 1931

The excellent first-half form in the league continued when Ayr were beaten at Fir Park. Willie McFadyen (4), Alan Craig and John McMenemy got the goals.

WEDNESDAY 22nd NOVEMBER 1944

Bobby Graham was born in Motherwell on this day. However, he started his football career with Liverpool when he left school and made a brilliant debut, scoring a hat-trick. He moved to Coventry City and Tranmere Rovers before arriving at Fir Park in the mid-1970s. After a quiet debut at Arbroath he finished top scorer in his first season but probably became better known for being the partner of Willie Pettigrew even though his own goal tally was respectable.

SATURDAY 23rd NOVEMBER 1935

Motherwell's dominant spell in Scotland was coming to an end but they were still strong. Tom Wylie, Bobby Ferrier and Ben Ellis saw off Hibs 3-2 at Easter Road.

TUESDAY 23rd NOVEMBER 1999

After the first game was rained off, justice was done at the second attempt when Motherwell defeated Hearts. It was heading for a draw when Pat Nevin collected a loose ball wide in the box and fired his shot into the top corner four minutes into injury time.

WEDNESDAY 24th NOVEMBER 1965

Tom Boyd was born in Glasgow in 1965. Despite being right-footed he played at left-back and developed into a full Scotland international. He also had the distinction of being only the second Motherwell captain to lift the Scottish Cup before he moved to Chelsea for £800,000 – a then record fee.

SATURDAY 24th NOVEMBER 1984

Despite John Gahagan's goal at Kilbowie, Motherwell slipped to defeat against Clydebank. Tommy McLean's side had coped well with relegation to the First Division and were soon on the road to promotion back to the top flight.

SATURDAY 25TH NOVEMBER 1922

A hat-trick from Hugh Ferguson and singles from Willie Rankin and Bobby Ferrier were enough to defeat Clyde at Fir Park. The Bully Wee put up stern resistance but ultimately went down 5-3.

SATURDAY 26TH NOVEMBER 1892

The Scottish Cup started when Campsie visited Dalziel Park and they were soundly beaten 9-2. The unlucky losers then successfully protested against the state of the Dalziel pitch and a replay was ordered. This time Campsie did better but were still on the wrong end of the 6-4 score, and on this occasion the result stood.

SATURDAY 26TH NOVEMBER 1966

'Dixie' Deans was a great scorer during his time at Fir Park and grabbed a hat-trick in the 6-2 win over Dunfermline. Willie Hunter (2) and George Murray got the other goals but Motherwell were fading from the time of the Ancell Babes and they would finish in the lower half of the table once more.

SATURDAY 26TH NOVEMBER 1983

Bobby Watson returned to Fir Park as manager but things didn't get off to the best start. The side went down 2-1 to Hibs and Watson would struggle as the side spent the season fighting an ultimately futile battle against relegation.

SATURDAY 26TH NOVEMBER 1994

A wonderful performance from Motherwell saw Partick Thistle dismantled at Fir Park. While the final result was only 3-1 Motherwell played beautiful football and could easily have run up a much higher score. One goal, finished by Billy Davies, came at the end of an 11-pass move which covered nearly the whole length of the park.

SUNDAY 27TH NOVEMBER 1977

All ten branches affiliated to the Association of Motherwell Supporters' Clubs took part in a five-a-side tournament organised by the Bellshill YMCA. 'Well stars Peter Millar and Stewart McLaren acted as referees while director Bill Dicke was on hand to give out prizes. Lanark defeated East Kilbride on penalties in the final.

SATURDAY 28TH NOVEMBER 1981

The First Division was proving to be easy meat for Davie Hay's high-scoring side and Dunfermline Athletic were next to be put to the sword. The club finished with 92 league goals and six of them, scored by Willie Irvine (2), Graeme Forbes, Stuart Rafferty, Johnny Gahagan and Brian McLaughlin, came in this convincing victory.

SUNDAY 28TH NOVEMBER 1999

A double was completed against Celtic with a 3-2 win at home. The much-maligned Derek Townsley scored a smart goal just before half-time by cutting inside his man and Don Goodman poked home the winner from close range after the break. Motherwell were now in fourth place, just one point behind Dundee United.

SATURDAY 29TH NOVEMBER 1924

It's hard to imagine but Airdrie were once the top dogs in Lanarkshire. In front of 8,000 fans at Fir Park they won 5-1 in a season they finished runners-up. Motherwell finished eighteenth of twenty.

SATURDAY 30TH NOVEMBER 1968

Brechin City visited Fir Park for the first time in the Second Division. However, their day out was not one to remember as hosts Motherwell won comfortably with goals from Jackie McInally and Jumbo Muir.

TUESDAY 30TH NOVEMBER 1993

Motherwell had already made a good start to the season and Tommy McLean strengthened the squad by signing Tommy Coyne for £110,000. Unfortunate personal circumstances meant Coyne was looking to return to Scotland from Tranmere Rovers and the Irish international became a crucial part of the side. He stayed for five years and became Motherwell's ninth-top post-war scorer in the league.

SATURDAY 30TH NOVEMBER 1991

The Motherwell programme contained an attack on *Glasgow Evening Times* columnist Tam Cowan. It suggested he should start writing articles based on facts and questioned whether he was a Motherwell fan at all. Cowan's credentials as a Dosser have since been well-established and he remains a popular writer and broadcaster.

MOTHERWELL FC
On This Day

DECEMBER

SATURDAY 1st DECEMBER 1934

Motherwell racked up one of their highest-ever scores when they defeated Dunfermline 9-3 at Fir Park. McFadyen scored four, Stevenson three with Duncan Ogilvie and John McMenemy netting the others.

SATURDAY 1st DECEMBER 1984

Meadowbank Thistle were one of the youngest clubs in the Scottish League and Motherwell visited their Commonwealth Stadium for the first time in 1984. It proved a disappointing trip as the team were beaten 4-2 despite goals from Rab Stewart and Johnny Gahagan.

SATURDAY 1st DECEMBER 1990

St Johnstone returned to the top flight with a shiny new stadium which was, at this point, one of the most modern in the country. Motherwell's first visit to McDiarmid Park ended in a 2-1 defeat.

SATURDAY 1st DECEMBER 2001

This day had one more first visit when Motherwell travelled to Livingston – the latest incarnation of Meadowbank. But, once again the match was not worth remembering as the side went down 3-1 although James McFadden's glancing header showed his potential.

SATURDAY 2nd DECEMBER 1961

Wins at Tynecastle have not come that frequently over the years for Motherwell, but one cracker occurred in 1961. A Pat Delaney hat-trick was backed up by a double from Pat Quinn and one from Bobby Roberts as the hosts were swept away 6-2.

SATURDAY 3rd DECEMBER 1932

Prolific striker Willie McFadyen added another five goals to his tally in an exciting 6-3 win over Third Lanark at Fir Park. Willie Moffat grabbed the other goal in front of a crowd of 4,500.

SATURDAY 3rd DECEMBER 1977

Despite Willie Pettigrew's goal at Pittodrie, Aberdeen ran out comfortable 4-1 winners over Motherwell. This would turn out to be Willie McLean's last match in charge of the team as the side had been on a dismal run featuring just one win in the previous 11 games.

FRIDAY 4TH DECEMBER 1998

Tragedy struck Fir Park when youth player Andy Thomson died of a heart complaint. The game against Dundee the following day was postponed as a mark of respect for the 19-year-old.

WEDNESDAY 4TH DECEMBER 2002

A run of eleven games, which produced only one point, saw Motherwell sink to the bottom of the table but the team hit back against Hearts. The Jambos had no answer to a sensational performance and lost 6-1 having trailed 4-0 at half-time.

SATURDAY 5TH DECEMBER 1981

Under Davie Hay the goals never seemed to stop flowing. East Stirlingshire were next to be crushed by the Motherwell juggernaut as they lost 6-0 at Firs Park.

SATURDAY 6TH DECEMBER 1913

Motherwell lined up in chocolate brown kit for the only time in their history, due to a colour clash at Hearts. An unspectacular draw provided little reason to use the kit again for superstitious purposes.

SATURDAY 6TH DECEMBER 1958

Motherwell were saved by fog at Celtic Park when the game was abandoned with the hosts leading 2-0. Visibility was so bad, those in the press box were not sure it was Charlie Aitken who went in goal when injury forced keeper Hastie Weir to move to outside-right after the break! The replayed match ended 3-3 in January 1959.

TUESDAY 6TH DECEMBER 1977

After a dreadful run of form left the side flirting with relegation, Willie McLean resigned. Assistant John Haggart was appointed caretaker.

SATURDAY 7TH DECEMBER 1996

Celtic were defeated 2-1 in an exciting game at Fir Park. Despite leading, things looked grim when Jamie Dolan had to replace the injured Scott Howie between the sticks but he kept his goal intact until losing an 83rd minute equaliser. Ian Ross prodded home a last minute rebound to secure a dramatic win.

SATURDAY 8TH DECEMBER 1923

A few months after being signed, inside-forward George Stevenson made his debut in a 2-1 loss to Third Lanark. Stevenson helped the club to the top of Scottish football and to win the 1932 title.

SATURDAY 8TH DECEMBER 1984

After a deal with the car dealership was agreed earlier in the week, Motherwell wore Ian Skelly on their shirts for the first time in the draw with Airdrie.

FRIDAY 9TH DECEMBER 1921

Archie Kelly was born in Paisley on this day in 1921. He was a huge success for Hearts before he moved to Fir Park via a spell at Aberdeen. Goals in both 1950s cup final victories followed and aside from his tremendous scoring talent, he was popular with the fans due to his fantastic work rate. He left to join Stirling in 1953.

SATURDAY 10TH DECEMBER 1921

Hugh Ferguson scored all five of Motherwell's goals in a 5-2 win over Clydebank as he continued his impressive form – he had also scored both goals in the previous match, a 2-0 win over Partick Thistle.

SATURDAY 10TH DECEMBER 1949

Motherwell claimed their record victory against Rangers when they tore through the 'Iron Curtain' defence at Fir Park. Kelly's double paved the way and further goals from Willie McCall and Jimmy Watson delighted the 29,000 crowd.

SATURDAY 10TH DECEMBER 1966

'Dixie' Deans was a great scorer but developed disciplinary problems. His first red card came in a 4-2 defeat against Celtic but further dismissals against Dunfermline, Aberdeen, Clyde, Hamilton and Stoke followed before he was sold to Celtic for a cut-price £17,500 in 1971.

SATURDAY 10TH DECEMBER 2005

Falkirk finally left the dilapidated Brockville and Motherwell visited their new out-of-town ground for the first time in December 2005. Jim Hamilton headed the only goal of the game.

SATURDAY 11TH DECEMBER 1971

Motherwell received a hiding when they went down 8-3 away to Partick Thistle. Thistle had just won the League Cup in sensational fashion against Celtic and would go on to finish in seventh spot in the table, ahead of Motherwell in tenth. The side were initially competitive but a sensational half-hour spell from the Jags blew Motherwell away.

TUESDAY 12TH DECEMBER 1978

The search for a new manager ended when Ally McLeod was persuaded to leave Ayr United to take over at Fir Park. McLeod had led Scotland to the 1978 World Cup but though he inspired Motherwell to an early unbeaten run, the writing was already on the wall as the club struggled in vain against relegation.

SATURDAY 13TH DECEMBER 1958

There would come a time several decades later when wins at Aberdeen became rarer than hen's teeth but that was not an issue on this day. Ian St John scored twice as the team cantered to a simple 4-0 win.

WEDNESDAY 13TH DECEMBER 1961

Motherwell were involved in the Scottish Cup early in season 1961/62 and Dundee United visited Fir Park in mid-December. John McPhee (2), Bobby Young and Willie Hunter scored the goals which defeated the visitors 4-0 as Motherwell began a run which would take them all the way to the semi-finals.

SATURDAY 14TH DECEMBER 1963

Despite enduring a season of mid-table mediocrity in the league, Motherwell could still produce the occasional entertaining game. Goals from Bert McCann (2) and Willie Hunter produced a 3-3 draw with Rangers in front of a 16,501 strong crowd at Fir Park.

THURSDAY 15TH DECEMBER 1977

After advertising the vacant manager's position in the national press over the previous weekend, the board sifted through applications and drew up a shortlist. Bertie Auld, the ex-Celtic Lisbon Lion who was managing part-time Partick Thistle, was viewed as one of the early favourites to get the job.

MONDAY 16TH DECEMBER 1929

The Scottish Football Association wrote to the club to provide guidelines for arranging foreign tours. The club was told they had to request permission from the association to agree games, at least a month prior to departure.

FRIDAY 16TH DECEMBER 1932

Three years later it was the turn of the club to write to the SFA. Secretary Sailor Hunter composed the letter detailing proposed fixtures for a summer tour of Denmark, including matches against Aarhus and Odense. A sign of the times was that the club's letterhead contained a swastika in the header, a commonly-used greeting symbol.

SATURDAY 17TH DECEMBER 1955

The juniors were a ripe source of talent for Motherwell and Pat Quinn was spotted playing at the lower level. He was snapped up after impressing for Bridgeton Waverly against St Rochs and enjoyed an excellent period with the Ancell Babes at Fir Park.

FRIDAY 17TH DECEMBER 1971

The *Motherwell Times* gleefully reported praise for the match programme in a review. One of their former reporters was the editor of the *Fir Park News* which the *Scotsman* said was 'heading in the right direction'.

SATURDAY 17TH DECEMBER 1988

Dundee were defeated 1-0 at Fir Park as Alistair Maxwell staked his claim to the number one spot. He had been at Fir Park for a few years before securing his place in the team but this was the first of 106 consecutive appearances, a run which ended with his 1991 cup final heroics against Dundee United, his last game for the club.

SATURDAY 18TH DECEMBER 1993

Motherwell's title challenge kept going with a comfortable 3-1 win over Dundee at Dens Park. Tommy Coyne already looked like an influential addition to the side and he made an excellent start to his Fir Park career. A double in this match gave him a very impressive five goals in his first five games.

SATURDAY 19TH DECEMBER 1959

Motherwell have not made many trips to Arbroath on league business and they have little cause to remember this one with fondness. Despite Pat Quinn's goal, Motherwell lost 3-1 at Gayfield to the side who finished last in the First Division.

SATURDAY 20TH DECEMBER 1997

Things took an upturn in the battle against relegation when Dunfermline visited Fir Park. Two second-half goals from poacher Owen Coyle gave the home side a much needed 2-0 victory.

SATURDAY 21ST DECEMBER 1895

Perhaps Motherwell would win in Glasgow more often if they had more opportunities. Port Glasgow resigned from the league in 1912 but by then had been involved in a number of battles with Motherwell. On this day they lost 4-3 to the Steelmen at their home ground, Clune Park.

TUESDAY 22ND DECEMBER 1936

An era ended as veteran striker Willie McFadyen was transferred to Huddersfield Town. McFadyen was one of the championship-winning players who would start to drift away as the 1930s progressed, but his departure did bring one familiar face back to Fir Park. He was swapped for Duncan Ogilvie who had been purchased by Huddersfield Town for £2,900 in March but failed to settle.

THURSDAY 22ND DECEMBER 1977

Roger Hynd was offered the role of manager following the departure of Willie McLean earlier in the winter. Hynd was the nephew of the great Bill Shankly but this stint at Fir Park was his only spell in management. He did enough to keep the team in the Premier League after taking over but resigned after failing to make progress in the next season.

SATURDAY 22ND DECEMBER 1979

When John Gahagan made his debut for Motherwell, it could only be from the bench. He would go on to make 93 substitute appearances for the club – a record – with the first of those coming in a 2-1 derby win over rivals Airdrie.

SATURDAY 23RD DECEMBER 1933

Motherwell's wonderful run at the start of the season came to an end just before Christmas when the side lost for the first time. Clyde won 2-1 at Fir Park to end an unbeaten stretch of 23 games as the team tried to regain the championship won in 1932.

SATURDAY 24TH DECEMBER 1966

The team were heading for a Christmas bonus when they were 3-1 up at home to Falkirk at Fir Park. However, the floodlights failed giving the Bairns a reprieve and they made the most of it by winning the replayed match 2-1 in April.

THURSDAY 25TH DECEMBER 1930

Sailor Hunter dropped Willie Dowall and recalled Willie McFadyen. This brought the famous forward line of Johnny Murdoch, John McMenemy, McFadyen, George Stevenson and Bobby Ferrier, which reaped an instant dividend: a 3-0 win over Partick Thistle.

SATURDAY 25TH DECEMBER 1971

Motherwell's last appearance on Christmas Day came at Bayview in 1971. A goal by Brian Heron secured a 1-1 draw as the team finished safely in the middle of the table, well ahead of East Fife who only just escaped relegation.

SATURDAY 26TH DECEMBER 1931

Motherwell suffered their last defeat of the season, as they lost 1-0 at Ibrox. The Steelmen soon regained the initiative in the title race.

WEDNESDAY 26TH DECEMBER 2001

Motherwell missed a glorious chance to solidify their SPL status when they lost at home to St Johnstone. A win for the 'Well would have put them eleven points ahead of the guests but the Saints won 2-1 to move within five of the 'Well above them.

THURSDAY 26TH DECEMBER 2002

Motherwell moved off the bottom of the table with a 1-0 win over Rangers. James McFadden scored the winner, as Francois Dubourdeau pulled off a string of fantastic saves to keep the visiting stars at bay.

SATURDAY 27TH DECEMBER 1958

Motherwell suffered only their second defeat of the season. Partick Thistle dismantled the side 4-0 at Firhill.

SUNDAY 28TH DECEMBER 1958

Terry Butcher was born in Singapore on this day. He became Motherwell manager as the club plunged into administration and crafted a combative young side that was popular with the fans.

SATURDAY 29TH DECEMBER 1951

Charlie Cox and Tommy Sloan both made their debuts in the win against Hibs. George Stevenson travelled to Tynecastle in the Christmas holidays in a successful attempt to sign them.

SATURDAY 29TH DECEMBER 2007

Motherwell defeated Dundee United but the result was overshadowed by the tragic death of Phil O'Donnell. The Motherwell captain collapsed on the pitch and died later in the evening despite being rushed to Wishaw General Hospital. Fir Park was turned into a makeshift shrine within hours as fans paid their respects by leaving shirts, scarves and notes in front of the Main Stand. The club soon announced the Main Stand would be renamed in honour of Phil.

THURSDAY 30TH DECEMBER 1948

Johnny Aitkenhead signed from Hibs for £5,400. He made his debut a couple of days later and became a fixture on the left wing, winning both domestic cup competitions with the club in the early 1950s.

SATURDAY 31ST DECEMBER 1994

Motherwell lost 3-1 at home to Rangers, losing ground in the title race. Things looked good when Paul McGrillen scored a brilliant equaliser after the break, but Brian Laudrup restored the lead and the win put Rangers clear of the Steelmen at the top of the table.

SATURDAY 31ST DECEMBER 2005

Terry Butcher's side ended 2005 with a last gasp win at Livingston. Richie Foran's goal had been equalised but Kevin McBride drilled into the bottom corner in injury time to secure an away victory.